Tsai-Shin Fong

The Persuasive Power of Rhetorical Website Design

Tsai-Shin Fong

# The Persuasive Power of Rhetorical Website Design

## Marketing Loyalty in the E-Commerce Environment: Rhetorical Concepts, Methods, Implements

VDM Verlag Dr. Müller

**Impressum/Imprint (nur für Deutschland/ only for Germany)**
Bibliografische Information der Deutschen Nationalbibliothek: Die Deutsche Nationalbibliothek
verzeichnet diese Publikation in der Deutschen Nationalbibliografie; detaillierte bibliografische
Daten sind im Internet über http://dnb.d-nb.de abrufbar.
Alle in diesem Buch genannten Marken und Produktnamen unterliegen warenzeichen-, marken-
oder patentrechtlichem Schutz bzw. sind Warenzeichen oder eingetragene Warenzeichen der
jeweiligen Inhaber. Die Wiedergabe von Marken, Produktnamen, Gebrauchsnamen,
Handelsnamen, Warenbezeichnungen u.s.w. in diesem Werk berechtigt auch ohne besondere
Kennzeichnung nicht zu der Annahme, dass solche Namen im Sinne der Warenzeichen- und
Markenschutzgesetzgebung als frei zu betrachten wären und daher von jedermann benutzt
werden dürften.

Coverbild: www.purestockx.com

Verlag: VDM Verlag Dr. Müller Aktiengesellschaft & Co. KG
Dudweiler Landstr. 125 a, 66123 Saarbrücken, Deutschland
Telefon +49 681 9100-698, Telefax +49 681 9100-988, Email: info@vdm-verlag.de
Zugl.: Lynn University, Florida, Diss.,2005

Herstellung in Deutschland:
Schaltungsdienst Lange o.H.G., Zehrensdorfer Str. 11, D-12277 Berlin
Books on Demand GmbH, Gutenbergring 53, D-22848 Norderstedt
Reha GmbH, Dudweiler Landstr. 99, D- 66123 Saarbrücken
ISBN: 978-3-639-08429-0


**Imprint (only for USA, GB)**
Bibliographic information published by the Deutsche Nationalbibliothek: The Deutsche
Nationalbibliothek lists this publication in the Deutsche Nationalbibliografie; detailed
bibliographic data are available in the Internet at http://dnb.d-nb.de.
Any brand names and product names mentioned in this book are subject to trademark, brand or
patent protection and are trademarks or registered trademarks of their respective holders. The use
of brand names, product names, common names, trade names, product descriptions etc. even
without
a particular marking in this works is in no way to be construed to mean that such names may be
regarded as unrestricted in respect of trademark and brand protection legislation and could thus
be used by anyone.

Cover image: www.purestockx.com

Publisher:
VDM Verlag Dr. Müller Aktiengesellschaft & Co. KG
Dudweiler Landstr. 125 a, 66123 Saarbrücken, Germany
Phone +49 681 9100-698, Fax +49 681 9100-988, Email: info@vdm-verlag.de

Copyright © 2008 VDM Verlag Dr. Müller Aktiengesellschaft & Co. KG and licensors
All rights reserved. Saarbrücken 2008

Produced in USA and UK by:
Lightning Source Inc., 1246 Heil Quaker Blvd., La Vergne, TN 37086, USA
Lightning Source UK Ltd., Chapter House, Pitfield, Kiln Farm, Milton Keynes, MK11 3LW, GB
BookSurge, 7290 B. Investment Drive, North Charleston, SC 29418, USA
ISBN: 978-3-639-08429-0

# ACKNOWLEDGMENTS

There are many people who played a key role in the completion of this book, and to them I would like to offer my appreciation.

First, I would like to express my appreciation to Dr. Frederick L. Dembowski and Dr. Grodzki Erika. Thanks Dr. Dembowski for giving many essential methodological advices for this book. Thanks Dr. Grodzki Erika for her helpful advice, direction and support during the entirety of my research.

I am also thankful to my parents and my parents-in-law. Thanks them for their consistent love and support through the years of my research. Specially thank my husband Yi Lin Yu for his love, wisdom, and encouragement. Without him, I would not have embarked this adventure.

Finally, I would like to thank VDM publisher for giving me a chance to make this book public.

# TABLE OF CONTENTS

# TABLE OF CONTENTS
## Continued

## CHAPTER IV: RESULTS

## CHAPTER V: SUMMARY, DISCUSSION, IMPLICATIONS, FURTHER RESEARCH, AND CONCLUSIONS

**TABLE OF CONTENTS**
**Continued**

## LIST OF TABLES

**LIST OF FIGURES**

Page

# CHAPTER I

## INTRODUCTION

Chapter one introduces information pertaining to the persuasive power of rhetorical website design: marketing loyalty in the E- commerce environment. Included are introductions to the background of the research, statement of the problem, purpose of the research, research questions, importance of the research, objectives of the research, research design rationale, limitation of the research, contribution of the research, and structure of the book.

### Background of the Research

For the past few decades, the transition to increased reliance on computer systems has affected many industries in the world. The development of the Internet, and particularly the World Wide Web, has generated a strong impact on marketing world wide. Undoubtedly, the Internet transforms businesses into diverse processes. A number of new types of online trade models have become the alternative to traditional markets. Among the various online trades, Business-to-Consumer (B2C) e-commerce is growing in popularity. The technological trends fuel new ways of doing business, and the Internet technology is certainly the key to a profound transformation in business (Gutterman, Brown & Stanislaw, 2000).

It is unquestionable that any type of improvement in technology would generate certain effects on human lives. The Internet technology is not just revolutionizing business, but also fundamentally changing the way people communicate with each other, and gathering information around the world. Computers are an integral part of our lives. Sterne (2001) specified the Internet provides enormous potential benefits for people worldwide. Many of the things we do in our daily life we can do on the Internet. The number of users "clicking on" websites has increased considerably. Indeed, Internet users are growing exponentially, faster than any other media (Stallings, 2001). One recent study by Computer Industry Almanac, 259 million online users worldwide were expected to increase in 1999, and the number is now expected to increase over 765 million by year-end 2005 (Commerce Net, 2002).

Bill Gates stated that electronic commerce will be enlarged because the usage of personal computer is growing rapidly (Joyce, 2001). With an enormous multitude of potential consumers globally, the Internet offers an opportunity that merchants have never before seen. Many companies understand the Internet is one of the critical factors to their future success and survival in businesses. Today, more and more people are shopping online, and the numbers of purchases that they are making each year may increase. In 2001, Forrester Research reported that the growth of purchasing online went from $7.8 billion U.S. in 1998 to $45 billion U.S. in 2000. In other words, online shopping grew an incredible 580 percent between 1998 and 2000. Forrester Research further forecasted that the world Internet economy may reach between $1.4 trillion and $3.2 trillion by 2003 (Cordy, 2003).

The Internet is unique in that it is a global information network that is everywhere. A networked world can offer tremendous possibilities for doing business more efficiently and profitably (Bishop, 1998). In the Internet commerce, buyers and sellers greatly depend on Internet market-related activities to conduct their business. The aim of a marketing strategy is to sell more products and generate more profit. Certainly, the Internet creates a more facilitating environment that confers a benefit for global participation (Mann, 2002; Wolak, 2001). Companies can benefit online by exploring cost saving, understanding the principles of disintermediation, gathering more information, and entering the global market. Additionally, the interactive nature of the Internet can be an excellent opportunity to develop deeper and long-term consumer relationships (Newell. 2000; Sindell, 2000; Sterne, 2001). These advantages are directly associated with Internet technology and the interactive nature of the medium (Rutter & Southerton, 2000).

There is an important difference between traditional and electronic commerce in the temporal elements of shopping. The Internet allows conducting business without distance and time barriers. Some consumer behavior scholars define the convenience of online shopping as saving time and effort, including physical and mental effort (Wolfinbarger & Gilly, 2001). Bishop (1998) mentioned that the Internet market is spatial in nature; all marketing stages can happen at the same time. Through the Internet, consumers can deal directly with companies without intermediaries. On the other hand, companies can move from mass marketing to direct marketing.

Hall (2001) indicated that one of the big opportunities afforded by the Internet is the ability to break through geographic constraints. Therefore, physical locations are no longer the only concern in making business decisions. Additionally, there is no time limit to make a trade in the Internet market. The Internet can be accessible 24 hours a day, 7 days a week. Consumers can keep shopping in a virtual mall when traditional stores are typically closed. By removing the time constraints of a store, the continuous accessibility of the Internet makes online shopping a convenience to consumers everywhere. Consumers can complete online transactions anywhere they want via the Internet. This efficiency is one of the strengths brought by the online selling format. Eventually, the Internet has led to a critical mass of consumers and marketers participating in a global online marketplace (Bishop, 1998; Braddock, 2001; Capodagli & Jackson, 2001; Fiore, 2000; Plant, 2000). That is the power of Internet commerce.

## Statement of the Problem

Online commerce has captured the special attention of marketers for many years because the Internet allows merchants to do business with more customers for less money. Companies are aware of this change and are willing to adapt to such change because they think they can take advantage of digital technology (Harrison-Walker, 2002). Unfortunately, old models of marketing do not totally apply to the new media, because the Internet marketing environment is essentially different than the traditional business market (Carroll & Brodhead, 2001; Hall, 2001). Indeed, failures of Internet commerce are possible. The Internet provides great potential opportunities to the marketers while creating serious challenges.

The major challenge to companies is that electronic consumers have different characteristics than traditional consumers. The electronic consumer is a special type of consumer for Web-based marketing. E-consumers tend to be more active than common traditional consumers (Sterne, 2001). E-consumers can select exactly the information they want from millions of Web pages by using powerful search engine technology. Unless E-consumers want to access to your website, they can ignore it without difficulty

3

(Rutter & Southerton, 2000). The Web itself is designed to empower users. As a result, if E-consumers find that a certain website is not a welcome place to stay, they will leave the site and never return (Coney & Steehouder, 2000; Easley, 2002).

Robinson, Tapscott and Kalakota (2000) indicated that the basic concepts for online shopping and online purchasing share similar attributes with the traditional shopping and purchasing. Once people become aware of a product, they often become desirous of that product. Before the advent of the Internet, people might have forgotten their desire for something not available locally; with the Internet, people can now simply "point and click" their way to purchases (Reiss, 2000). However, while it is true that individuals are in general eager to do business on the Internet, this enthusiasm does not necessarily translate into success for any particular business. The connection between the desire of people to acquire goods not locally available to them in as cheap and convenient a way as possible, and the success or failure of any particular company, is based in large measure upon the quality of the design of the company's website (Cato, 2001; Garrett, 2002; Sachs & McClain, 2002; Smith, 2000; Sindell, 2000).

Generally speaking, a company's website is a unique communication medium to effectively implement their business on the Internet. The online seller lacks the physical embodiment that allows a face-to-face look at the merchandise. Consumers primarily rely on the visual impact of websites design. Thus, e-vendors need to have brilliant Web design strategies to persuade consumers to buy. In marketing strategy, many companies understand that consumers' satisfaction and loyalty are essential to their success; however, few companies know how to create an effective online shopping site that can promote consumer satisfaction, and then facilitate the completion of online purchases or repeat purchase behaviors.

Hwang (2000) illustrated that many online sellers spent 25 to 50 percent of their budget on advertising in order to attract new online buyers. Newell (2000) advocated that it costs from five to ten times more to acquire a new consumer, than it does to make another sale to an existing customer. If a company uses $40 to attract a new consumer and the gross margin is 20 %, it means the company use $40 to acquire $37 in business (Smith, 2000). That is really not a smart marketing strategy while a firm spends money on promotion. The high costs of enticing new consumers are wasted if consumers come

4

to visit companies' site just one time, and never come back. The aim of marketing is to persuade consumers to come back often, and stay longer on the site, because this is the way to drive profits. If an e-commerce website can provide consumers with pleasant experiences and keep them satisfied, trust and loyalty can be easily built. On the other hand, websites not designed with consumer perspectives in mind are at high-risk for losing consumer loyalty.

A study by Braddock (2001) showed that only 0.04 percent of all websites have 80 percent of all consumer visits. It means to design websites; companies really need to combine theoretical and practical strategies that can attract the largest consumers as possible. In the virtual environment, the central question to marketers is how to create a site that enables their consumers to easily make online purchase decisions (Gutterman et al., 2000). The endeavor of website design is to create a welcoming buying environment to discourage the chance of "clicking away" (Bunnell & Richard, 2000; Haig, 2001; Pal & Ray, 2001). Novak, Hoffman, and Yung (1999) argued that consumer experience in an online environment is a critical issue to create advantage on the Internet. Actually, there is not a second chance to win consumer loyalty; therefore, companies need to ensure each contact creates a positive experience from the customer's viewpoint (Newell, 2000). Many website designs, however, make consumers confused and frustrated in the virtual stores, because many designers have a lack of knowledge about what the consumer desires. If consumers cannot find what they want, or have a bad experience on a website, it is very difficult to persuade them to come back again.

The other challenge to companies is that no matter how big or small, companies have the same ease of access to potential consumers (Grant, 1999; Isidro, 2002; Pal & Ray, 2001; Plant, 2000). It is now possible for a one-person, highly specialized firm to use the Internet to break down many of the marketing and distribution barriers that for years have limited small companies. With skilled use of the Internet, a small company can have a global clientele – just as a multinational corporation reaches around the world to find its consumers. The lower start-up costs of Web presence minimize barriers entry into Internet commerce, which has created more trade competitors worldwide.

Stewart and Zhao (2000) noted that the Web provides an essentially different environment for marketing activities than traditional media. Taking advantage of the

Internet to bring in new business involves the challenges of developing new strategies and new business process design. For years, the Internet as a commercial medium has caused marketers to experiment with innovative ways of marketing to consumers in computer-mediated environments. Although the attractiveness of the online shopping, there are few studies to direct a firm's Web design strategies.

Several years ago, in order to face the rapidly changing electronic business world, many believed that the familiar axiom "if you build it, they will come" was the simple way to profit online. Corporate giants to small businesses invested large amounts of money in the Internet boom of the early to mid 1990's. Then we witnessed the rise and fall of many dot.com companies. A recent research study indicated that only 36 percent of pure online sellers have profitable online business (Quick, 2000). Of course, owning a company was actually never that simple. But the picture now is even more complicated since virtual stores have entered the picture. Part of what makes engaging in e-commerce so difficult is that there are no paths that others have walked before one (Hall, 2001; Bunnell & Richard, 2000). And the costs of making mistakes in the field can be substantial: A badly designed website can make all the difference, not only for a single sale, but also for the entire future of a company (Newell, 2000).

The Web presence looks simple, but creates vast challenges for many marketing organizations. Consequently, the worn principle "if you build it, they will come" is not true anymore (Colby, 2002). The new technology provides unlimited opportunities for selling products online; however, is not a panacea to companies in cyberspace, if the marketers do not pay attention to new approaches to design their websites.

To continue moving forward, businessmen must transform some of their perceptions of e-commerce to avoid mistakes made by the first generation of dot. comers. An important issue related to e-commerce is what factors would facilitate consumer loyalty to a website. To successfully launch an e-commerce website, the question is not as simple as "if we build it, will they come?" but "if we build it, will they be loyal to the site?" Smith (2000) advocated that building loyalty is tough because it takes two willing people to build a relationship. In fact, consumers like to have a relationship with a company, only if this firm can win their trust and respect. The loyal consumers are willing to visit over time, promote, and become involve with companies' site (Culter &

6

Sterne, 2001). How do businesses attract the millions of Wed users, and establish a continuing relationship with them in the virtual world? It is a complicated job.

The basic problem is how one website out of the thousands that now exist can attract consumers and satisfy the needs of consumers through websites. This book, therefore, attempted to investigate one of the most important elements of e-commerce, the importance of website design. This book examined the design factors on a website that can affect consumer loyalty in the electronic shopping malls.

Consumer loyalty is an important concept in electronic commerce. In fact, consumer loyalty has been widely discussed in the research for many years; a considerable amount of literature has been devoted to the consumer loyalty issues in the brand or product allegiance (e.g., Brown, 1953; Jacoby & Chestnut, 1978; LaBarbera & Mazursky, 1983; Roellig, 2001; Schultz, 2001). However, the marketplace has changed quickly over the past several years, since the advent of the public World Wide Web in 1992. Many previous approaches that addressed consumer loyalty in traditional business settings, may be not appropriate in an electronic environment, where shoppers have various choices to products and brands, and are not be restricted by time or geography. Actually, there been little empirical research conducted dealing with loyal issues in the Internet shopping environment. It is the time for us to examine, and define, a new loyalty approach in the Internet commerce for the $21^{st}$ century marketplace.

In today's crowded virtual marketplace, it is not so much how companies communicate with consumers, but how, and in what ways, the consumer wants to contact companies. E-vendors need to have right tools to win the fierce battle (Smith, 2000). Many researchers (Newell, 2000; Sindell, 2000; Smith, 2000) declared that the more often a shopper visits a website, the more likely that consumer will spend an increasing amount of money on the site. Ultimately, it can establish loyalty and generate more profits for the online retailers. An effective website design could be one of the guaranteed ways to a company success, because the website is the major contact that consumers have with the company in the virtual environments (Haig, 2001; Sterne, 2001; Winn & Beck, 2002). The benefit of an enticing and dynamic company website can increase the quality of customer service, decreasing the time between the initial contact with a customer and the closing of a sale, simplify both marketing and sales processes, and expanding the pool of customers (CustomerCentric, 2002; Deck, 2001).

This book examined the rhetoric of websites, arguing that creating an enticing website is possible for any business that attends to a set of fundamental rules of rhetoric. The aim of persuasive Web design is to change consumers by motivating them to think, feel, or act differently. To do that, a website needs to offer consumers reasons that can convince them to visit and purchase repeatedly. A well-designed website can help close a sale, can help persuade a consumer that this is the place and the time to buy (May, 2000). Website designs that utilize rhetorical strategies to create a welcoming buying environment will have better opportunity to discourage the chance of "clicking away". Websites need to have rhetorical ability– to persuade their consumers by logos, pathos, and ethos. By surveying consumers who have used websites recently as a way to buy goods, this book helps to illuminate some of the basic dynamics of e-commerce, problems that have not been sufficiently studied yet, in part, because the phenomenon is itself so new.

## Purpose of the Research

One purpose of this research was to determine the extent an enticing website design affects selling goods to individual consumers. These members of an increasingly globalized society are increasingly aware of the goods and services that are available to them. In other words, this book examined the degree to which a persuasive website design, as opposed to other business elements, is responsible for the overall success, or failure, of an e-commerce firm. In addressing this question, the researcher must necessarily answer another question, which is how one defines a "well-designed" website. Is such a definition to be made in purely economic terms, and if so, how? Therefore, this researcher attempted to highlight the importance of a website design based on the consumers' perspective. The virtual environment is a consumer-driven marketplace. Many believe that the secret to online success is marketing from outside-in approach (Haig, 2001; Plant, 2000; Schultz & Kitchen, 2000). An outside-in approach will help companies meet online marketing goals, and build long-term relationship with consumers. This means companies need to pay attention to what the consumers really desire, instead of what companies have created in the past. An effective website design should have the persuasive power to motivate and influence consumers' purchase intention. This book can show how to design a persuasive website through theories and systemic methods.

The other purpose of this research was to show how design elements affect the visual persuasion in e-commerce websites. The basic assumption underlying the approach was that consumers' intentions to make repeated visits, and purchases on their current website, is determined by the rhetorical function of persuasion in the design elements of a website. In the increasingly competitive world of e-commerce, marketers should understand the important connection between website design and consumer loyalty.

This book investigated some of the complexities of conducting business in our virtual age, focusing on e-commerce, but also asking how the presence of e-commerce on the market has affected traditional businesses as well. Although there are many different ways to examine consumer loyalty, this implemented a rhetorical approach to understanding customer allegiance in the Internet commerce. This book presented a framework which is grounded in the classic rhetorical concept of logos, pathos, and ethos, which addressed companies examining the website design in Business-to-Consumer (B2C) Internet Commerce, and the unique characteristics of their customers.

## Research Questions

The aim of this book was to explore the key factors that may explain the persuasive power of website design on consumer loyalty in Business-to-Consumer (B2C) Internet commerce; and how Aristotle's three methods of persuasion (i.e., logos, pathos, and ethos) may combine to create a viable, living, reproducible paradigm for 21$^{st}$ century consumerism. The findings of this book are likely to make a significant contribution to the future design of e-commerce websites, due to the in-depth analysis of the characteristics that are inherent in a persuasive Web design.

This book investigated online consumers' attitudes and perceptions regarding website design from a classic rhetorical theory approach. Specially, the researcher sought to determine how certain a set of independent variables affect a particular dependent variable. The major independent variables used in the research were (1) Logos, (2)

Pathos, and (3) Ethos. The dependent variable was Consumer Loyalty. The central question addressed by this book was how to design a persuasive website, which is able to convince consumer to purchase products, and return to purchase over and over again in an e-commerce site.

The specific research questions for this book were as follows:

(1) What is the relationship between rhetorical elements (i.e., logos, pathos, and ethos) and consumer loyalty in e-commerce website s?

(2) What visual design elements and effectiveness constitute a persuasive model on a website?

(3) Do males and females have different preferences in regard to visual design elements on a rhetorical website?

(4) Will different age groups have diverse preferences for rhetorical elements (i.e., logos, pathos, and ethos) on a website?

## Importance of the Research

As electronic commerce continues to grow throughout the world, the demands for greater knowledge about designing a highly persuasive website on the new electronic based Internet marketing will continue to increase. However, many reports have showed that online business is "all hype and no profit" (Quick, 2000). Despite the fact that millions of dollars were lost, e-commerce has once again caught the attention of the general public, as well as businesses. Marketers and designers are eager for hints to help them to win the intense battle. Experts emerged from the ashes and attempted to develop new paradigms designed to explain the failure, redirect the quickly amassed skills and resources previously applied, and stem the exit of great numbers of commercial entities from the Internet and a "virtual economy".

Many previous research studies on Internet marketing issues have focused on the techniques; few studies have shed light on the visual design elements of websites for marketers. On the other hand, there is a large body of literature on website design, but not many studies take the theme of the rhetorical function of website design into consideration. Although these earlier studies did demystify some factors that drive the success of e-commerce website, they failed to at answer what is needed persuade or influence online consumers' experience of willing to visit, purchase, and become loyal toward a website.

The primary importance of this book is that it analyzed website design separate from other aspects of e-commerce. Distinguishing website design has been neglected in previous studies. This research used powerful and established rhetorical tools that allowed the researcher to disentangle website design from other factors in an innovative way. This approach was a dynamic one, which not only explains the current state of e-commerce, but also future changes in the field. The expectations of consumers who buy online change over time – and change far more quickly than consumers using brick-and-mortar stores (traditional stores). The rate of change overall in the technological world is commensurate to the rate of change in the expectations of those who buy online (Christopher & McKenzie, 2003; Robinson, et al., 2000). While an electronic shopping cart was sufficient to satisfy, and even delight consumers only a few years ago, consumers now are interested in far more sophisticated, flexible, and personalized tools to conduct virtual commerce (Mountain Media, 2003).

In the online shopping environment, there is the disadvantage to the consumer in his or her inability to check the quality of goods without examining them directly (Braddock, 2001; Colby, 2002; May, 2000). Consumers are negatively affected when they are unable to "experience" a purchase prior to making it. The Internet presents a unique challenge to compensate for the lack of sensory data normally demanded by the consumer. Designers have been largely unsuccessful in adapting to this gaping chasm of expectation vs. actuality of experience with disastrous results in commerce, financial, and business ethic arenas. Problematic is the lack of sensory input when making purchasing decisions; a traditional consumer evaluation involves seeing, touching, sampling, "trying on", smelling, hearing, and even tasting before actually making the purchase (Mary, 2000; Winn & Beck, 2002; Stewart & Zhao, 2000). Once these samplings and sensory evaluations have been made (pathos), this consumer can then rely on the logical reasons for visiting a particular store (logos) and consider the reliability of the manufacturer (ethos) when deciding to spend the money.

Given both the globalization of the economy, and increasing business dependence on e-commerce, the effectiveness of website design is a key question both for those in businesses and for consumers. Since websites are often the main contact with consumers in the Internet market, a company's website elements may include some persuasive components that have an impact on consumers' positive experience. To evaluate what design elements constitute the persuasive power for the customers to have positive experience on a website, it is expected that increased levels of the consumers' positive experience would lead consumers to have more optimistic attitudes toward websites, stronger purchase intention, and loyalty. If consumers "feel good", marketers can have a better chance to win the battle on an e-commerce website (Coyle & Thorson, 2001; Lynch, Kent, Gillete & Srinivansan, 2001).

To understand how the task of merchandising can be translated from the world of selling real products, to real people, in face-to-face encounters, into an electronic based Internet market. In a virtual world, none of the traditional tools and cues of live encounters exists, requiring one to understand the ways in which humans communicate with each other, and the ways in which different kinds of information interact with each other. Traditional forms of marketing and selling products tend to scream rather than whisper. It is not appropriate to the Internet commerce, because consumers often use the Internet in their own homes; they want websites that are in many ways more intimate than traditional forms of selling. They do not want to feel that their "personal space" has been invaded by the more obvious forms of consumer activities (Van Duyne, Landay & Hong, 2002). Consumers do not want either a "pretty" website or a standardized one. They want a simple but flexible, and powerful site that can satisfy their desire (Mountain Media, 2003; Smith, 2000).

This book investigated the connections between the rhetorical underpinnings of website discourse, and the effectiveness of these sites in drawing individual consumers to do business with their companies. It is meaningful to investigate consumer loyalty in Business-to Consumer (B2C) Internet commerce from a rhetorical perspective because persuasive variables might play an important role in affecting individual perception and intention to become loyal toward an e-commerce website. The researcher relied on the results of questionnaires, as well as analysis of the websites to determine their effectiveness along several different vectors. website design has to go beyond the merely informational and persuasive, to be entertaining and viscerally appealing.

## Objectives of the Research

Launching a site with a bad design may be waste of money, since it will not attract and retain consumers. Besides, websites are the main contact with a public audience; a poorly-designed website can seriously damage the reputation of companies (Steehouder & Coney, 2000). In order to succeed, companies need to learn from both the victories, and mistakes, of others from e-commerce history. It is very important that marketers can follow some critical website design rules when they spending time and money on building websites. In this book, the researcher suggested that when designing a website, a rhetoric perspective approach can be more effective to consumers than a purely technological perspective. Those wishing to use the Internet as an effective business tool must create a selling strategy that takes into account the specific nature of the medium. For example, people do not "read" hypertexts that appear on a computer terminal in their bedroom in the same way that they "read" the information presented about a product in a store. While this seems to be quite common sense, it does not mean that the ways in which websites should be designed to meet these differing needs is a simple task.

The current literature does not reveal comprehensive answers about the important design factors as influences on the Business-to-Consumer (B2C) e-commerce websites. The objectives of this research are to provide a road map, suggesting ways in which both consumers and companies can use websites to their best advantage, by subjecting these sites to rhetorical analysis.

Specific objectives of the research are:

1. To propose a conceptual framework is based on Aristotle's rhetorical theory, which is modified by adding a set of design variables affecting customers' intention to become loyal toward an e-commerce website.

2. To examine how strong these convincing design variables on a website could influence customer loyalty.

3. To broaden our understanding about the visual impact of design elements on websites.

4. To enhance our comprehension of customer loyalty in Business-to-Consumer (B2C) Internet context.

5. To promote our knowledge of a well-designed website from consumers' perspective.

It is a difficult job to realize how traditional selling techniques work, and to comprehend how these techniques can be translated to new media and new markets. This understanding requires a rhetorical analysis of the rules of communication that obtain in both traditional selling encounters and website s. An analysis of the ways in which we construct communication, and the ways in which websites can be constructed, both to reflect traditional forms of selling and communication, as well as novel ways of exchanging information and goods – is at the center of this research.

## Research Design Rationale

The theoretical foundation for this research was established through the literature review of pertinent research. The review included identifying relevant research in the areas of website design, e-commerce strategy, World Wide Web marketing, consumer loyalty, and practices of rhetorical theory and consumer-centered design.

This research intended to extend Winn and Beck's research taxonomy (2002) by using a quantitative research method (survey questionnaire) to further measure human experience of consumerism; therefore, the dependent variable – consumer loyalty. The study by Winn and Beck (2002) was the first to attempt incorporating all three rhetorical elements, and apply them to commercial website design, by using the qualitative method (interview and direct observation). Winn and Beck recruited 15 subjects who had previous buying experience on the Web in their study. Their study showed that subjects had directly reacted to the site's design during their interaction with the interface, and the subjects ensured that there were varying degrees of persuasion, by the way that the salient factors were presented on the site. Although Winn and Beck's study showed us these salient factors could have varying degrees of persuasive power to consumers, they did not investigate whether these factors could truly have an influence on the revenue of an e-commerce website.

In order to answer the research questions of this research, the investigation focused on thirteen independent variables and one dependent variable. The independent variables are each linked to one of the three rhetorical modes that Winn and Beck (2002) outline.

14

Four of these independent variables are linked to Winn and Beck's concept of logos, or logic. These variables are price, variety, product information, and effort. Three of the independent variables are linked to Winn and Beck's concept of pathos, or emotion. These variables are playfulness, tangibility, and empathy. Four of the independent variables are linked to Winn and Beck's concept of ethos, or credibility: recognizability, compatibility, assurance, reliability. Finally, two demographic variables: age and gender. The dependent variable is consumer loyalty, which is a measure of the good faith of consumers to a website. Loyal consumers would frequently visit, make repeated purchases or service, and make "word-of-mouth" referrals to the same website.

Visual design is the logical persuasive power influencing online consumers to buy from virtual stores. Using the previously unapplied concepts of logos (appeal to the logic), pathos (appeal to the emotions), and ethos (appeal to the credibility) to electronic commerce as found in the research taxonomy of Winn and Beck (2002), this book revealed an appropriate melding of the consumer's perception of a positive online experience with a satisfying visual experience.

The research design employed a quantitative method approach using closed-ended questions on survey instruments. The survey consisted of 36 closed-ended questions, plus an open-ended question at the end. The researcher asked respondents to rate the questions based on a closed-ended 1 to 9 Likert scale format. By employing a 1 to 9 Likert scale, the researcher intended to make all of the variables to be continuous variables. The survey was distributed by the researcher to consumers, who have previous experience with online product purchases in the U.S. The researcher sent e-mails to potential respondents inviting them to participate in a Web survey. A non-probability sampling (convenience sampling) method was used. Data was conducted in a period of four months from September to December of 2005 in the U.S. This research sample consists of 307 participants (154 males and 153 females).

Collected data were analyzed by SPSS Windows Version 11.0. The techniques for data analysis included: descriptive statistics, correlation analysis, independent-samples $t$ test, one-way ANOVA analysis, and multiple regression analysis. The level of statistical significance was set at $p < = .05$. Results from this survey provided the insight and perspective to make the important strategy, quality, and operational decisions that are necessary for effective e-commerce implementation. By understanding what people want when they purchase online, marketers can do a better job providing services, and improving the quality of website design.

## Limitations of the Research

Researcher's limitations factored into the results of the findings of this research; presumably there is a "perfect" research model for quantitative research of this nature, but time and resource limitations prevent the active search for the method. This research was subject to several limitations. It is important that readers are aware of these limitations at the outset. First, a longitudinal study can provide consumers' crucial information over time. However, the intense follow-up interview, or conducting a long and in-depth research project, is not practical in this research, due to severe time limitations.

Second, the researcher lacked sponsorship to obtain a bigger sample size from population. This limitation forced the research study employing a convenient sampling method to choose participants for the survey. However, the cost of using a convenient sampling method is the risk of bias, sampling error, and limited generalization of the findings to any larger population.

Third, this research focused only on the persuasive power of rhetorical website design in the Business-to-Consumer (B2C) Internet context. The results of this research cannot be accurately projected to other industries.

## Contribution of the Research

The fact is that there is not a comprehensive established theory in the area of persuasive websites design available presently in the e-commerce context to date. Many previous studies focused on the technological aspect of website design, or based entirely on the opinions of experts, rather than on the results of empirical research; however, these kinds of approaches may result in low-quality website, if designers do not fully understand some theoretical background before they create a website. Little research directly addressed the issue of the persuasive power on influencing online consumers' experience of willingness to purchase and loyalty.

16

This book focused on factors that are extremely important from both theoretical and practical perspectives. The researcher proposed a theoretical framework based on a modified theory of Winn and Beck's study (2002) that includes three means of persuasion to explain how a website's visual design elements may influence consumer loyalty. The book is valuable because it offers many website firms a model to explain why consumers are willing to return the same website.

The purpose of this research was to investigate empirically-based principles that Web designers can employ to improve the likelihood that consumers will be happy to visit and be loyal with a site. The objective of this research was to provide another layer to the literature from which other research programs and focuses can spring.

The outcomes of the research are likely to be significant to Internet commerce, consumers, and researchers. Web developers, consumer-oriented websites, and companies with heavy Internet-reliance for market share results, will benefit greatly from increased quantitative and qualitative research into this area. For example, Web designers and engineers can use quantitative findings to better understand how to build a Web portal, or business presence, on the Internet designed to "capture" loyal and responsive consumers or clients, based on the visual impact of elements that work.

The aim of this book was to gather, synthesize and present the current finding on website design from consumers' perspective. It is believed that by examining the relative importance of these rhetorical variables in affecting consumer loyalty, this research would contribute not only to better understanding how customer allegiance is formed, but also to effectively managing it from a marketer's standpoint.

## Structure of the Book

This book is organized as follows:

Chapter one introduces the research into the persuasive power of rhetorical website design: marketing loyalty in the e- Commerce environment. This chapter identifies the background of the research, research questions, and the purpose, objective, importance and contribution of the book. Chapter one also notes the limitations of the research.

Chapter two provides a review of the literature of key studies and concepts in this research area. The major gap is the limited amount of empirical literature investigating the consumer loyalty of website design.

The research methodology is discussed in chapter three. Chapter three begins with a discussion of the research questions and design. The sampling plan, instruments, procedures and data collection methods, reliability and validity of the research, evaluation of the ethical aspects of the research, and methods of data analyses are presented.

Chapter four reveals the results of the statistical analysis of the survey instrument. All findings relevant to the research are present in appropriate tables, figures and graphic.

Finally, chapter five summarizes the research findings. It discusses theoretical and practical implications of the results. Strengths and limitations of the research are analyzed and discussed. This chapter also provides the conclusion, recommendations, and suggestions for further research.

Appendices present the e-mail invitation letter, the information and informed consent statement for Web participants, the consumer loyalty questionnaire, institutional review board approval, the result of correlation coefficient among eleven sub-independent variables, ANOVA analysis: descriptive information of each age group, and the open-ended question: comments by subjects.

# CHAPTER II
# REVIEW OF THE LITERATURE

## Overview

Chapter two provides a review of the literature of key concepts in this book. All pertinent literature has been reviewed for this topic in order to facilitate the theory development for this research. This scholarly review of earlier study provides an appropriate history and recognizes the priority of the work of others. This review focused only on literature and conclusions directly relevant to the subject and the problem addressed in the book.

Chapter two begins with a historical look at the development of Internet commerce, including a relevant literature review of the differences between traditional commerce and Internet commerce, a common goal between traditional commerce and Internet commerce, the benefits and challenges to companies and consumers using Internet commerce, the important role of website design in e-commerce context, and the important role of consumer loyalty in e-commerce context. Also reviewed are the theoretical foundations for this book included identifying relevant research in the areas of practices of rhetorical theory and consumer-centered design.

Chapter two presents a conceptual framework for thinking about how companies might study the website design for Business-to-Consumer (B2C) Internet Commerce and the unique characteristics of the consumers they serves. Taken together, chapter two is to integrate the current findings from both website design and marketing literature in Internet context. Marketing managers evaluating the success of their websites and marketing academics interested in teaching a module on e-commerce should benefit from this review.

# A Historical Look at the Development of Internet Commerce
## Technical Development of the Internet

*The Creation of ARPANET*

In 1957, the Soviet Union launched the first satellite. The effect in the United Stated was shock! Eisenhower instantly established the Advanced Research Projects Agency (ARPA) to regain the technological lead in the arms race.

Meanwhile, researchers discovered a way to bundle information into structures called packets. In 1969, the Advanced Research Projects Agency developed ARPANET as an operational packet-switching network. Packet-switching means a method of transmitting message through communications network (Stallings, 2001). The ARPANET connected various military and research sites. The main purpose of this network was to make sure all computers can build reliable networks without intrusiveness (Cremel, 2001).

Computers were added quickly to the ARPANET during the following years; however, in the ARPANET model, the network was not reliable enough; any portion of the information could disappear at any moment across the network. In 1970, the Network Working Group (NWG) developed the initial ARPANET Host-to-Host protocol, called the Network Control Protocol (NCP). The NCP can allow dissimilar computer systems to communicate and transmit data across a network. Before that time, the user had to physically carry magnetic tapes or punched cards to transfer data from different computers (Cremel, 2001).

In 1971, there were 23 host computers linked with each other by ARPANET. However, a more international and standard protocol was needed in order to make the network (Hammer, 1998). In 1974, ARPA researchers developed a standard language that can interconnect different networks. They developed IP (Internet Protocol) technology which defined how electronic messages were packaged, addressed, and sent over the network. This was known as a transmission control protocol/internet protocol (TCP/IP). TCP/IP allowed users to link with various branches of other complex networks directly (Gromov, 2001). The ARPANET soon came to be called the Internet.

The original idea of the Internet was for communication within the military. In 1972, ARPA researchers employed a new program to send messages over the net. This program allowed person-to-person communication directly that we now refer to as e-mail. In 1984, the National Science Foundation (NSF) had created a similar network called NSFNet, which provides a major backbone communication service for the Internet today (Cremel, 2001). The NSFNet use the TCP/IP technology developed from ARPANET and established a distributed network. It connected the centers with 56,000 bits per second telephone lines; and had the ability to transfer two typewritten pages per second (Stallings, 2001). Academics researchers, government agencies, and international research organizations began to use the network; however, in 1990, ARPANET was shut down by the Defense Communications Agency, due to limited funding and support from the military. Ultimately, NSFNet supplanted it as the main high-speed transmission line (Hammer, 1998).

The Internet was based on the concept of connecting multiple independent networks together. The Internet, as we know now it, embodies a key underlying technical idea and an open architecture networking. However, Stallings (2001) explained that the early Internet was used by computer experts, engineers, and scientists. There was nothing friendly about it. Users had to learn to use a very complex system.

In 1986, the NSFNet developed a cross country 56 Kbps backbone for the Internet. The National Science Foundation worked hard to set rules for its non-commercial government and research users. As the commands for e-mail, FTP, and telnet were standardized, it became a lot easier for non-technical people to learn how to use the net. Sterne (2001) illustrated that while there were prior difficulties, it did open up the use of the Internet to more people. Indeed, the NSF's effort enhanced the possibility of everyone having access to the network in the future.

In 1989, another significant event happened in making the nets easier to use. Tim Berners-Lee at the European Laboratory for Particle Physics (CERN) proposed a new protocol for information distribution. This protocol, which became the World Wide Web in 1991, was based on hypertext – a system of embedding links in text, which can link to other text. The innovation allows academic researchers to find ways to communicate with other researchers or organizations around the world and to share valuable files and resources together (Stallings, 2001).

By the 1990's, business discovered the Internet; the network was opened to a few commercial sites (AT& T Technology, 1995). Since the Internet was initially funded by the government, it was originally limited to research, education, and government uses. Commercial uses were not allowed, except when they served the goals of research and education. This policy gradually stopped around the early 1990's, when independent commercial networks began to grow (Stallings, 2001). It then became possible to route traffic across the country from one commercial site to another without passing through the NSFNet Internet backbone. After that, many ".com" companies appeared on the Internet; and the Internet users grew explosively. Indeed, the Internet has revolutionized the computer and communications world like nothing before (Stallings, 2001).

*From the Internet to the World Wide Web*

The original World Wide Web (WWW) concept was designed in 1989 by Tim Berners-Lee and scientists at CERN. By the end of 1991, Berners-Lee developed a line-oriented browser/editor program, and had coined the name World Wide Web for the program. The World Wide Web is released free on an ftp (file transfer protocol) site; however, this program is limited to a population used. In the fall 1992, Mark Andreason of NCSA (National Center for SuperComputing Applications, Illinois) developed the graphic-based browser Mosaic. This is the first browser that had the ability to incorporate graphical information, which can provide the mechanism for user-friendly access (Sterne, 2001; Stallings, 2001).

Mosaic freed "the Web" from a DOS-like, text-based format. This gave birth to the Web. Mosaic was developed to run on UNIX X11 workstations, Macintoshes and Microsoft Windows personal computers. From that time, Web pages have had the same appearance on all computers, and the browser operated in a similar manner on all computers. This meant that WWW applications became independent of the computing platform used.

In 1993, Mark Andreason launched the other version- Mosaic X. By 1994, thousands of Mosaic had been installed on computers throughout the World. The potential of creating attractively graphical websites lead the Web to whole new audiences (Zimmerman, 1997).

Michael (2000) stated that the main difference between the Internet and the World Wide Web is that, "the Internet is a collection of computers connected by a huge network and general communication protocols. The World Wide Web is one of applications running across the computers on the Internet." (p.11). Stallings (2001) further defined World Wide Web as: "The Web is a system consisting of an internationally distributed collection of multimedia files supported by clients (users) and servers (information providers)." (p.104). The Web is based on the technology called HTML (Hypertext Markup Language), and the Web appears as pages that contain buttons or hypertext links to other pages when viewed by a Web Browser.

Typically, the linked text is blue or underlined when displayed; it can link to other documents, which may be text, files, and pictures. Basically, these pages are connected through a mechanism called a Universal Resource Locator (URL) that allows the links from one page to other pages on locally, or on distant computers worldwide. When users search the Internet, the Hypertext Transfer Protocol (HTTP) is a particular protocol that can help to search and retrieve in the World Wide Web. The HTTP is an address of a website that can allow people to call up the precise website or document for reviewing. Generally speaking, on the Net, the connections are between different computers; however, on the Web, the connections are between various hypertext links (Michael, 2000).

### Size and Growth of the Internet and the World Wide Web

Since the Internet is so vast in nature, it very difficult to determine its size at a given moment (Gromov, 1995). However, it is unquestionable that the Internet has experienced astonishing growth in recent years (Capodagli & Jackson, 2001; Hall, 2001; Hoffman, Thomas & Chatterjee, 1995; Stallings, 2001; Sterne, 2001). Consider this: It took 38 years for 30% of U.S. households to have a telephone; 17 years to have a television; 13 years to have a computer. However, the World Wide Wed has only taken less than 7 years to reach for the 30% of the United States. This is really a truly notable story of the

20th century, and positively shows that the Internet will continue to expand throughout the 21$^{st}$ century (Wolf, 1999).

*The Growth of Internet Hosts and Domains*

Wolf (1999) pointed out in 1981 that fewer than 300 computers were linked to the Internet, and by 1989, the number was less than 90,000 computers. By 1993, over 1,000,000 computers were linked. In 1995, there were 9,400,000 host computers world wide. Hosts refer to the number of machine addresses as reported by the name servers; however, this count does not include the people who own personal computers to access Internet. The Table 1 shows the gradual growth of Internet hosts and domains from 1993 to 1996 (Network Wizards, 1996).

Table 1

*The Gradual Growth of Internet Hosts from 1993 to 1996 (Network Wizards, 1996).*

| Date | Hosts | Domains |
|---|---|---|
| Jan 96 | 9.5 million | 240,000 |
| Jul 95 | 6.6 million | 120,000 |
| Jan 95 | 4.9 million | 71,000 |
| Oct 94 | 3.9 million | 56,000 |
| Jul 94 | 3.2 million | 46,000 |
| Jan 94 | 2.2 million | 30,000 |
| Oct 93 | 2.1 million | 28,000 |
| Jul 93 | 1.8 million | 26,000 |
| Apr 93 | 1.5 million | 22,000 |
| Jan 93 | 1.3 million | 21,000 |

Network Wizards (1996) indicated that as of January, 1996, there were 9.5 million host computers on the Internet. This number of hosts approximately tripled from January 1994 to 1996. The number of domains is also impressive; of these 9.5 million hosts,

24

240,000 are .edu or .net domains. The number of domains has been roughly tenfold from January 1993 to January 1996. This showed that many universities, companies, or other groups were already connected to the Internet around 1996. A domain name is any name representing any record that exists within the Domain Name System (i.e. com, nw.com, www.nw.com). The figure 1 shows the gradual growth of Internet hosts and domains from 1969 to 2002 (Zakon, 2003). The figure 2 shows the gradual growth of Internet domain from 1994 to 2008 (ISC.org, 2008).

Figure 1

*The Gradual Growth of Internet Hosts from 1969 to 2002 (Zakon, 2003).*

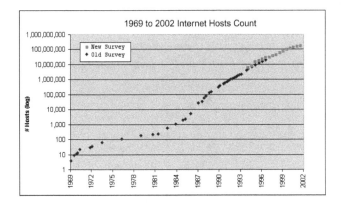

Figure 2

*The Internet Domains from 1994 to 2008 (ISC.org, 2008).*

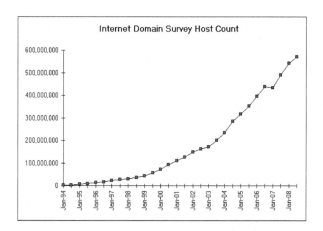

*The Growth of Internet Users and WWW Users*

The growth of the Internet population is even more remarkable. According to *Computer Economics*, an expected 213 million online users worldwide by 2001 and by 2005, the number is expected to increase to 350 million (Commerce Net, 1999). However, Computer Industry Almanac optimistically expects there will be 165 million on-line users in the U.S. by 2002, and over 490 million and 765 million users worldwide by 2002 and 2005, respectively (Commerce Net, 2001).

The figure 3 illustrates the Internet connectivity worldwide (Landweber, 1997). The figure 4 shows the Commerce Net (2001) forecasted the Internet growth worldwide from 1998 to 2003. The figure 5 illustrates the expected growth of Internet usage in U.S. from 1995 to 2005 (Commerce Net, 2001).

Figure 3

*The Internet Connectivity Worldwide (Landweber, 1997).*

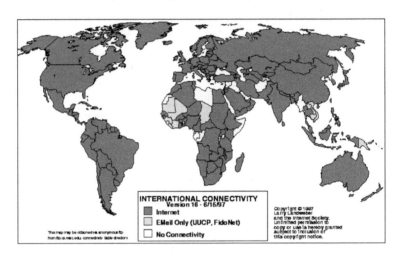

Figure 4

*The Expected Internet Growth Worldwide from 1998 to 2003 (Commerce Net, 2001).*

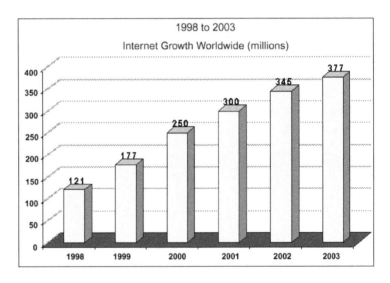

Figure 5

*The Expected Growth of Internet Usage in U.S. from 1995 to 2005 (Commerce Net, 2001)*

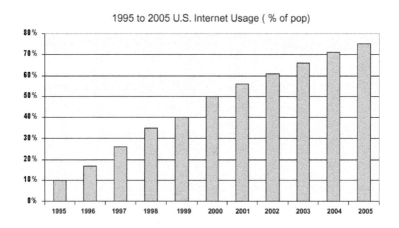

The Internet users in the U.S. and Canada also grew speedily. The Internet demographic survey report by Commerce Net (1999) showed that in 1997, 17% of online users (over the age of 16) in the U.S. and Canada; in 1998, 26% of online users; as of 1999, there were 92.2 million Internet users in U.S./Canada; and there were 73.3 million WWW users (over the age of 16 ) in U.S./Canada. These data clearly showed since 1997, there were 59% increase in Internet users; and 46% increase in WWW users.

The Table 2 shows the gradual growth of WWW and Internet users from 1995 to 1999 in the U.S./Canada.

Table 2

*The Gradual Growth of WWW and Internet Users from 1995 to 1999 in US/Canada*
*(Commerce Net, 1999).*

| Comparison of Internet and WWW population (million) | | |
|---|---|---|
| *Date* | *WWW Population* | *Internet Population* |
| 1995 | 14.3 | 22 |
| 1996 | 25.9 | 37.8 |
| 1997 | 50.2 | 57.8 |
| 1998 | 68.4 | 78.6 |
| 1999 | 73.3 | 92.2 |

*The Growth of Websites*

The growth of websites is even more exciting than that of the Internet. Gray (1995) estimated that for the second half of 1993, the Web had a doubling period of less than 3 months. There were 130 websites in 1993. In 1995, there were more than 23,000 websites. Additionally, the percentage of commercial websites has increased dramatically. Today, commercial activity on the Web has increased to the point where hundreds of new companies are adding Web pages every day. The Online Computer Library Center (OCLC) stated that the Web contained almost 8.4 million individual sites in 2001, compared to 7.1 million in year 2000 (Pandia, 2001). According to Pingdom.com annual report, there are above 162 million websites on the internet in 2008. The figure 6 shows the growth of websites from 1990 to 2008 (Pingdom.com, 2008).

Figure 6

*The Growth of Websites from 1990 to 2008 (Pingdom.com, 2008).*

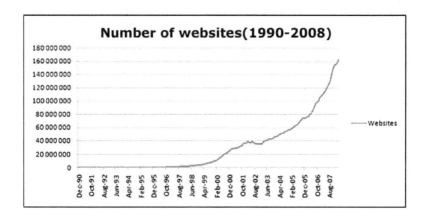

### From WWW to Internet Commerce

There are two basic reasons that lead to the prosperous development of Internet commerce. The first reason is faster computers and the second reason is the electronic mail (e-mail).

*Faster Computers*

The Internet is one of the youngest and fastest growing media in today's world (Hall, 2001; Hiag, 1998; Stalling, 2001; Sterne, 2001; Stewart & Zhao, 2000). The Internet is unique in that it is a global information network that is decentralized. Carroll and Brodhead (2001) explained the word "internet" literally means "network of networks". In itself, the Internet consists of thousands of smaller local networks scattered throughout the globe. However, when the Internet spread to worldwide, the concept of speed was a critical issue. The Internet needs speed; 14.4 modems can not do good jobs for loading colorful images, animation, or large text files. The rapid revolution in computer hardware truly facilitated the Internet, which owns more power than other communication system day by day (Michael, 2000). By regular phone lines, or speedy cable modems, people can have a fast access network system without painful waiting. Additionally, lower cost for computers and Internet access is another issue that has affected Internet usage (Michael, 2000). Since the prices of computers and related Internet fee have decreased, far more people are able to visit websites, and the number still continues to grow. Ultimately, there is buying and selling of goods online – this is the concept of e-commerce.

*The Electronic Mail (E-mail)*

Several researchers (Capodagli & Jackson, 2001; Gutterman, Brown & Stanislaw, 2000; Michael, 2000; Newell, 2000; Sterne, 2000; Stewart & Zhao, 2000) specified that the Internet is not just technology; it also provides an innovative way of doing business. Indeed, a networked world will offer tremendous possibilities for doing business more efficiently and profitably.

Lots of different kinds of programs can be used in the Internet. However, electronic mail (e-mail) is the most popular Internet activity worldwide (Hamman, 1998; Sterne, 2001). Electronic mail (e-mail) can send and receive message in seconds, and one message can be sent to many individuals at the same time. It is a powerful communication process for people. The e-mail's role in business is just like a telephone or a fax machine. Although the Internet is not the only way for businessmen to connect with each other, it obviously is the most useful method to maintain local, regional, national, and international communication (Hoffman, Thomas, & Chatterjee, 1995).

Furthermore, the e-mail also can serve as a communication channel for consumers to connect with companies' computers without human intervention. Consumers can contact companies anytime and anywhere, although they can not meet face-to-face. Colby (2002) mentioned that the e-mail marketing strategy could serve an important role in a successful e-commerce venture. The Internet is a reasonable alternative for conducting business without distance and time barriers. That is the power of e-commerce. Sterne (2001) illustrated that as e-mail is becoming such an increasingly important channel; e-commerce has the potential to be a money and time saver for both buyers and sellers.

### Electronic Commerce

E-commerce (electronic commerce or EC) is one of the most current issues in business today. Many businesses, large and small, have made e-commerce a priority (Saloner & Spence, 2002). What is electronic commerce? The Merriam-Webster Dictionary defines e-commerce as: "the buying and selling of commodities: in essence, trade." The definition of e-commerce by High-Tech Dictionary as: "E-commerce may include the use of electronic data interchange (EDI), electronic money exchange, Internet advertising, websites, online databases, computer networks, and point-of-sale (POS) computer systems." Southern and Janson (2000) defined e-commerce as: " the purchases of goods, services or other financial transactions in which the interactive process is mediated by information or digital technology at both, locationally separate, ends of the interchange." (p.139). For present purposes, we can define e-commerce quite simply as "doing business electronically" (Dunt & Harper, 2002). The activities can include gathering information about, communicating with, and trading with customers and suppliers through the World Wide Web (Anonymous, 2001). Generally speaking, e-commerce is the buying and selling of goods and services on the Internet, especially the World Wide Web (Colby, 2002).

E-commerce is a subset of electronic business. Dunt and Harper (2002) explained the different types of e-commerce as:

> E-commerce is generally classified as either business-to-business (B2B) or business-to-consumer (B2C). Some analysts identify government-to-business (G2B) and government-to-citizen (G2C) transactions as part of e-commerce but most definitions, including that preferred by the OECD, place government communications beyond the realm of electronic commerce. (Dunt & Harper, 2000, p.328).

Plant (2000) defined business-to-consumer (B2C) as: "… an electronic-based marketplace through which a retail customer wishing to make a transaction interacts with an organization." (p.24). In general terms, Business-to-Consumer (B2C) is the most recognized form of e-commerce, which includes online purchasing and other relevant electronic transactions that stress the direction of delivery from business to consumer (Kalakota & Whinston, 1997). The Internet gives a new way for consumers to make

32

purchasing decisions. Consumers have more information and additional alternatives to choose their products from the Internet.

Business-to-Business (B2B) e-commerce allows organizations to derive efficiencies from their supplier relationships. B2B is an ongoing partnership among participating companies. The Internet can help companies build strategic alliances, and improve the relationships between each other. As the results of Business-to-Consumer (B2C) and Business-to-Business (B2B) electronic commerce, business markets can become more convenient, but also more competitive than before (Grant, 1999).

### Online Shopping and Online Purchasing

Harrison-Walker (2002) stated that one of the big chances afforded to businesses is the Internet. It can be a great marketing channel to reach a global audience. For a thousand years, the buying and selling behavior of human beings has not changed markedly. As Terry (1999) noted that:

> Anthropologists claim that civilization began in earnest when our hunter-gatherer ancestors gathered together and began to trade with each other to gain goods and knowledge which could not be acquired from one's tribe. From here it was just quick jump to the formation of agrarian societies, villages and marketplaces- all outgrowths of mankind's propensity to try and make things easier on itself. (Terry, 1999, p.1)

Terry (1999) illustrated a similar goal in all online marketplaces as: "…bring people together who have something with others who want that something." (p.4). In the simplest terms, the purpose of the online marketplace is to bring buyers and sellers together to trade by way of the Internet. Therefore, the basic concepts for online shopping and online purchasing share the similar attributes with traditional shopping and purchasing (Robinson et al., 2000).

In the traditional world, if you go to shopping at a mall, you need to go to several stores and gather useful information to find a good price for a product. Once you decide to buy, you place the product in your shopping cart and pay money to the store's cashier. On the other hand, in electronic commerce, you seek information about a product or service you considering buying on the Internet, and you then place products you are

33

interested the online shopping carts. To pay online, you need to enter an online purchasing site to fill in a form with your shipping address and credit card number.

In general, online shopping provides the opportunity for consumers to visit different stores (websites) in search of merchandise for gathering useful information, and to further help him or her make a buying decision (Haig, 2001). An important part of the purchasing process for many consumers is gathering information, such as: product, pricing, and service before making a purchase. Indeed, the Web provides an efficient and effective means for doing so. The activity of online purchasing is one in which consumers decide to completely conduct the transaction through interactive online forms with companies on an online purchasing site. Purchasing involves the actual exchange of money for goods or services (Hijazi, 2000).

In the computer-mediated environment, e-commerce uses shopping metaphors to provide the similar experiences to consumers in the real world with the process of gathering product information and purchasing products (Coyle & Thorson, 2001). More and more consumers are willing to shop online because of the interactive nature of Internet. It can allow them an easier, and more convenient, way to shop for different products in a short time (Sterne, 2001).

Internet access has grown faster than any other communications technology in history. Pal and Ray (2001) stated that the Internet is changing the traditional marketing model and producing new business models. Eventually, e-commerce is evolving into the primary tool in conducting business transactions globally.

Forrester Research estimated the world Internet economy may reach $1 trillion dollars by the end of 2001. They also predicted that U.S. on-line spending would exceed $6 billion in 2001. Business-to-Consumer sales online amounted to $33.1 billion in 1999, a figure 120 percent greater than 1998 online sales revenues. By 2004, Forrester Research predicts that North America will lead global e-commerce transactions to $6.9 trillion. In the meantime, 60% of the world on-line population, and 50% of on-line sales will be made outside of the U.S. by 2003. Forrester now sets the global market at between $1.4 trillion and $3.2 trillion by 2003 (Cordy, 2003). Those aforementioned numbers illustrate that the Electronic commerce model is positive in relation to the growing market.

Today, commercial activity on the Web has dramatic and rapid changes; hundreds of new companies are adding Web pages daily. Pal and Ray (2001) mentioned that the Internet, and the ways it will be used, is only in its infancy. In fact, the buying or selling of goods and services on the Internet has not matured yet; it has just started, which indicates that Internet commerce has not reached its highest expansion period yet.

## Traditional Commerce vs. Internet Commerce
### *Overview*

The presence of e-commerce has introduced an entirely new way of doing business; it has also changed the manner in which traditional commerce is undertaken (Malone, Yates & Benjamin, 1989; Benjamin & Wigand, 1995). The Internet provides people a framework of businesses – using network to sell products and services to global consumers. Stewart and Zhao (2000) noted that the Web provides an essentially different environment for marketing activities than traditional media. In traditional commerce, buyers and sellers conduct business that without involving any Internet market-related activities. On the other hand, in the Internet commerce, buyers and sellers greatly depend on Internet market-related activities to accomplish their business.

The Internet has the ability to efficiently combine interactive content and commerce together. Many traditional merchants rush into the Internet market because they think they can take the advantage of digital technology (Harrison-Walker, 2002). Several years ago, in order to face the rapidly changing business world, many believed in the familiar axiom "if you build it, they will come" as the simple way to go about making a profit online. Unfortunately, old models of marketing do not totally apply to the new media, because the Internet marketing environment is essentially different than the traditional business market (Carroll & Brodhead, 2001; Hall, 2001). Indeed, failures of Internet commerce are possible. The Economist magazine (1999) reported that the top 25 Internet companies generated $ 5 billion in revenue and lost $1 billion. Of the new Fortune-50, 19 of them lost money in the recent years. The reports illustrated that the new technology can lead to higher profits; however, is not a panacea to some of the companies in cyberspace, if the marketers do not pay attention on new approaches in managing their

35

websites. Consequently, the worn standard "if you build it, they will come" is no longer true (Colby, 2002).

It is important for a company to understand that these two business models, traditional and Internet, have fundamental differences when it comes to determining appropriate strategies and effective website designs to attract consumers. By relevant review, the researcher differentiates the Internet commerce and traditional commerce in three dimensions: (1) traditional store vs. virtual store, (2) passive vs. active, and (3) unlimited time and borderless online market.

### *Traditional Store vs. Virtual Store*

The shift to e-commerce generates enormous challenges to online sellers. Certainly, when the connection we have to consumers is through interaction on a screen, marketers must pay attention to many issues that they take for granted in the face-to-face traditional stores.

In a face-to-face situation, salesmen are able to communicate in a multitude of ways with consumers. Conversely, the Internet requires a different set of skills. How do consumers face the virtual store? How does a company actually attract consumers in cyberspace? The Web can be described as a three-dimensional space with specific locations (Kevin, 1996; Sterne, 2001). The way that consumers conceptualize the Web is represented in the language and metaphors of website design (Marcus, 1993). For example, an online store on the World Wide Web is a virtual location where consumers can "click an icon", and then go shopping. When consumers use "a mouse" to click a cart icon on a Web page, it means to make a purchase. On the website, online buyers and sellers are manifested by hypertext, graphic, and animation on screen to comprehend information (Bishop, 1998). They cannot see the facial expressions, body language, or hear the tones and voices of the salespeople. When the selling process leaves the traditional store, many elements are left behind.

Marketers, just like their consumers, will need to have the ability to deal with a virtual selling environment in which they cannot see, hear, and touch the people with whom they are communicating. Cato (2001) stated that sense-making is an important issue in cyberspace environment. An effective websites design could be one of the guaranteed ways to company success, because the website is the major contact that consumers have with the company in the virtual environments (Haig, 2001; Sterne, 2001; Sachs & McClain, 2002; Winn & Beck, 2002).

### *Passive vs. Active: The Active Characteristic of E-consumers*

The electronic consumer is a special type of consumer for Web-based marketing. In the online shopping environment, or the electronic based Internet marketing, a dot.com seller delivers its product information or service by communicating with consumers through its website. Stewart and Zhao (2000) stated that electronic consumers have different characteristics in respect to traditional consumers. Bishop (1998) specified that Internet users belong to an elite group. They know their needs. The Internet users tend to be more active than common traditional consumers since the Internet presents an essentially different environment for shopping activities than traditional commerce (Sterne, 2001). Johnson-Sheehan and Baehr (2001) described Internet users as: "hunters and gatherers" in virtual space, "… they are hunting down specific information that will help them survive in a very complex world. Or they are gathering facts that help them solve problems." (p.23). E-consumers can select exactly the information they want from millions of Web pages by using powerful search engine technology. It means E-consumers have far more decision-making power to pull the information they want towards them from Internet, rather than exploring traditional media.

The passive trade does not work well for E-consumers in the World Wide Web market, since the Internet is a "pull" rather than "push" medium (Bishop, 1998; Sterne, 2001). In "push" media, such as television or brochure, the seekers are automatically provided information without much choice; however, in "pull" media, such as World Wide Web, the seekers express a need in order to receive specific information. In other words, the consumers select information that is of interest to them.

Hoffman, Thomas and Chatterjee (1995) indicated that the traditional marketing communication model for mass media is a one-to-many process; however, the Internet transforms the traditional model to be a many-to-many process. The one-to-many model is a passive model that corporations use to transmit content through a medium to a mass market of consumers. Figure 7 shows the traditional marketing communication model for mass media is one-to-many marketing communication (firms denoted by F; consumers denoted by C).

Figure 7

*Traditional One-to-many Marketing Communications Model for Mass Media (firms denoted by F; consumers denoted by C). (Hoffman, Thomas and Chatterjee, 1995)*

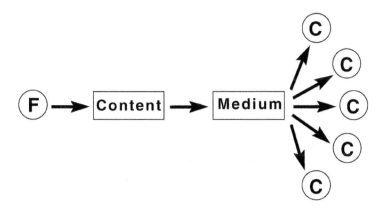

Hoffman et al. (1995) further explained that the traditional communication model may carry out the first two functions of the marketing model (i.e., provide a message to media, and disseminate a message to consumers). However, the unidirectional process of traditional mass media may restrain the persuasive function for differentiating a product or brand.

The new many-to-many model presents a "narrowcasting" phenomenon in which consumers can interact with the medium. It means consumers can interact with firms and other consumers. The content or information is not just provided from senders; yet, consumers can provide content to the medium. The computer-mediated environment is created by the individual consumer and firms together. Figure 8 illustrates the new many-to-many model is a radical departure on the Web (firms denoted by F; consumers denoted by C).

Figure 8

*A New Many-to-many Model of Marketing Communication. (firms denoted by F; consumers denoted by C). (Hoffman et al., 1995)*

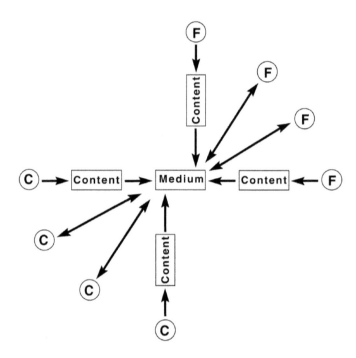

Coney and Steehouder (2000) emphasized that, "Indeed, the Web itself is designed to empower users to choose from a variety of roles offered them at a particular site, and to create their own meanings by following different pathways through the information." (p.329). Therefore, E-consumers are no longer constrained to their physical location; they can navigate the different virtual stores and pull what they want (Rutter & Southerton, 2000). Unless consumers want to access your website, they can ignore it without difficulty. Bishop (1998) indicated that there is no effective way to push dot.com sellers' business message to potential E-consumers. On the contrary, E-consumers will try to find you if your company's website can appeal to their specific needs and wants.

As a result, if E-consumers find that a certain website is not a welcome place to stay, they leave the site and never return.

The consumer, not the seller, will control the marketing system in the 21st-century global marketplace (Schultz & Kitchen, 2000). The role play of an E-consumer is no longer passive; it is much more active than before. If designers want their visitors to be fully engaged in their website, they must offer a great Web experience so that visitors are able and willing to stay. It is important for companies to understand the active characteristic of E-consumers when they determine a strategy to attract him or her. Certainly, E-consumers are extremely willing to come back over and over, if they feel satisfied with your website (Smith, 2000).

### *Unlimited Time and Borderless Online Market*

There is an important difference between traditional and electronic commerce in the temporal elements of shopping in the two media. While customers may only come to a traditional store when it is open, it is possible for them to shop without any temporal limits at all in an on-line arena. Of course, there are a number of stores that are open all night; however, these stores tend to receive the majority of their customers during traditional hours. As one manager of a Walmart store noted, while people are often eager to buy things at four o'clock in the morning, they generally would rather be able to do so from the comfort of their home rather than having to go to a store (Robbinson, Tapscott & Kalakota, 2000).

Generally speaking, the Internet can be accessible 24 hours a day, 7 days a week; there is no time limit to make a trade in the Internet market. In fact, the Internet allows consumers to keep shopping in the virtual mall when traditional stores are typically closed. By removing the time restraints of a store, the continuous accessibility of the Internet makes online shopping the most convenient for consumers.

Pal and Ray (2001) indicated that one of the big opportunities afforded by the Internet is the ability to break through geographical constraints. The Internet by nature is borderless; therefore, national or international boundaries are no longer the only concern in making a business decision.

The Internet allows individuals and businesses to establish remote presences, and to extend their reach into markets far beyond their physical location. In traditional commerce, the locations of companies had a certain influence on their marketing success; however, on the Internet, the business location of a company becomes almost unrelated for consumers' stopover (Pal & Ray, 2001). This means that a company's physical location is irrelevant to its Web presence on the Internet, including time zone and country, because Internet commerce is delivered to end-user via a computer using standard Internet technology. Goods and services can be ordered from any place where people can access the Internet.

As the market becomes borderless and without time limit, there are significant differences between doing virtual business and conducting business the old-fashioned way. Some of the most important differences between managing a traditional business and running a virtual one comes in the arena of marketing the product or services that the company offers (Capodagli & Jakson, 2001; Pal & Ray, 2001; Saloner & Spence, 2002). Marketers have to think about how well they can engage this market. The task for marketers in this new age is how to create an effective website to distribute information about their products and service. The content of websites needs to address the shared needs of consumers, regardless of the geographic areas where they are located (Sachs & McClain, 2002; Smith, 2000).

### A Common Goal between Traditional Commerce and Internet Commerce

The Internet has changed the business world in just a few years. Now, many companies are stores without walls and can exist in our real world such as: Amazon.com, Travelocity.com, and eBay. E-commerce owns the great ability for exchanges of goods and services. Despite the importance of those above-mentioned differences, it is also important to acknowledge the similarities between the two types of commerce.

In many ways businesses, both virtual and real, are more similar than one might initially suspect. All businesses are interested in selling goods or services, to members of the public, to make a profit for the owners and the shareholders. All successful businesses are capable of balancing innovation and entrepreneurial risk-taking with traditional and conservative business practices. All companies have to be aware of which

41

other firms are offering similar services or products, so that they can compete against them successfully – or decide to move into another market niche, rather than competing directly. All companies rely on receiving accurate information, both from within the company and from the larger market in which they operate (Gutterman, Brown & Stanislaw, 2000).

Newell (2000) stated that the marketing concept emphasizes the importance of satisfying consumers; the purpose of Internet commerce is not exceptional. In fact, E-consumers expect that they can earn the most value (i.e., goods or services) for their money. Although the rules of successful Internet commerce have not been clearly exposed yet, the principles that stress successful Internet marketing, are the same principles that underlie successful traditional marketing in general – to make consumers happy.

Winn and Beck (2002) explained the common goal between traditional and Internet commerce as:

> E-vendors and traditional retailers share a common goal: to lure customers to their stores, invite them in, show them their products in the most attractive manner, lead them to items they are looking for, call their attention to special sales and promotions, suggest additional buying options, and eventually facilitate the actual purchase (Winn & Beck, 2002, p.18).

In both traditional and Internet commerce, sellers need to find a way to attract consumers to their business places. The function of the website design is similar to that of a store display. The common goal is to generate awareness and positive attitudes toward the site (Novak, Hoffman & Yung, 1999).

In a virtual environment, face-to-face transactions can be replaced by faceless interactions across geographic borders. In virtual stores, websites are often the major opportunity to communicate with consumers. The cause-and-effect is simple; if the impression is not favorable, consumers will not stay to shop but "click away" quickly. Recker and Kathman (2001) clearly illustrated the importance of design, "… people are influenced by the stimuli around them. What is seen, heard, felt, and experienced encodes precepts that influence impressions, expectations, and ultimately behavior." (p.70). The design content of a site, such as layout and appearance, must achieve consumer satisfaction, because the website design is the main interface through which both marketers and consumers could interrelate. Websites are not designed with consumer perspectives in mind are at high-risk for losing consumer loyalty. On the other hand, websites that successfully meet consumer expectations significantly increase the likelihood that consumers will return to the site (Haig, 2001, 2000; Sindell, 2000).

In general, both the on-line business and the traditional one exist for the same goal: they want the consumer to spend money with them and not with one of their competitors. Because of this fundamental common goal, both on-line and traditional stores seek to offer their best possible combination of competitive prices, high-quality service and dynamic websites, while at the same time earning an acceptable profit.

## The Benefits and Challenges to Companies Using Internet Commerce
### *Overview*

Joel (1998) indicated that new technology can launch new business industries or elevate the existing ones. For example, the invention of refrigeration strengthened the meat industry, and the assembly line facilitated mass production of the automobile. Now, the Internet has had significant impact on businesses globally. The Internet today is the technical structure enabling people to gain access to the World Wide Web (WWW); however, in the early 1990's, an Internet business only meant a company that offered hardware and software necessary for individuals to use the Internet. Companies like AOL or Yahoo could only help users connect with their offices or friends. With a short decade, the World Wide Web has become the favored international mass medium. Companies rushed into the arena when they sensed the innovative market chance. Stallings (2001) asserted that computer networks make the world connected, and that this concept is applicable to global economy.

Digital technologies and worldwide networks are greatly transforming all aspects of business, and today, many companies can provide goods and services on the Internet (Saloner & Spence, 2002; Walton, 2002). It has been claimed that the Internet is the most exciting marketing innovation in history (Hall, 2001; Hoffman et al., 1995). Certainly, computers allow people to perform operational tasks more quickly and efficiently than ever before. Unrestricted by physical location, e-commerce opens up

43

tremendous potential benefits for companies. For instance, traditional companies (brick-and-mortar) can choose to have a presence on the Internet, because the Internet can expand their client base. Virtual companies (dot.com) can operate only on the Web (e.g., Amazon.com, eToy, and eBay) to create their new territory. New products, services and new relationships have come about because of the Internet. Many researchers (Pal & Ray, 2001; Rutter & Southerton, 2000; Saloner and Spence, 2002; Zhao & Steuart, 2000) advocated that online business is a growing phenomenon; indeed, online selling has captured the imagination of many merchants seeking to do business with more consumers for less money.

### The Benefits to Companies Using Internet Commerce

Marketing activities occur through different channels. The aim of a marketing strategy is to sell more products and generate greater profit. Stewart, Frazier, and Martin (1996) classified marketing functions into two types of channels: communication and distribution channels. Peterson, Balasubramanian, and Bronnenberg (1997) stated that all marketing functions can be carried out through three distinctive types of marketing channels: they are communication, transaction, and distribution channels. However, with an enormous multitude of potential consumers worldwide, the Internet offers an opportunity that merchants have never before seen.

This book categorizes companies' benefits with using the Internet from the perspective of cost saving, disintermediation, distribution channel, gathers information, global marketing, work environment, and consumer support. These advantages are directly associated with Internet technology and the interactive nature of the medium.

*Cost Saving*

Giga Information Group in 1999 estimated that the online business has saved $17.6 billion in 1998 for companies. They estimated that future business will save companies $1.25 trillion globally by 2002 (Grant, 1999). There are several cost saving benefits for business usage of the Internet. First, businessmen can use the Internet to connect global vendors and consumers faster and more efficiently. E-mail is a low cost method when compared to long distance telephone and mailing costs. For example, a USPO (United

Stated Postal Service) First class letter costs 37 cent when mailed in the US, so 1,000 pieces of mail sent to consumers would cost $ 370; however, with Internet tools, the same information costs 2 to 3 cents for each by e-mail, and people can receive information in seconds, rather than in days. The Internet technology provides a chance to easily reduce costs to complete business transactions (Heuberger, 2001; Vine, 1995; Wigand & Benjamin, 1995).

Another cost benefit to companies who use websites to sell their products or services is underselling their competitors (Pal & Ray, 2001; Sterne, 2001). In other words, e-commerce owners can usually offer their products or services to consumers at a lower cost than the owners of bricks-and-mortar (traditional) businesses (Microsoft. com, 2003). Additionally, e-commerce could provide 24 hours service without paying extra fees for salesmen. For Instance, a consumer wants to buy a digital camera in a virtual store. He or she can fill out a form describing the functions and features. Then the consumer hits a button and instantly receives a list of cameras, and their technical features, that best-matching his or her desired needs. Sachs and Mcclain (2002) explained that on the site, the recommender systems can provide "intimate" recommendations to a consumer, thereby filling the same role as a salesman.

Furthermore, e-commerce businesses offer corporate owners a high degree of flexibility, in terms of being able to offer new products, low overhead inventory practices, and associated holding costs (Saloner & Spence, 2002). Just-in-time inventory strategies are especially helpful to e-commerce businesses that do not have warehouses like traditional businesses. The low overhead of e-commerce is especially attractive to many businesses that effectively have a store that is open twenty-four hours a day, 365 days a year, and does not require an on-site staff, rate or mortgage, property taxes, insurance for the property and on-site employees, and has no physical upkeep or maintenance of a building (Web-design-uk. biz, 2002).

*Disintermediation*

Haig (2001) stated that, "one of the most radical effects of Internet is what e-marketers refer to as disintermediation. This basically means the end of the intermediary." (p.2). Bishop (1998) argued that the traditional marketing environment is linear in nature; however, the Internet commerce is spatial. In the traditional marketing environment, everything happens slowly and in a logical sequence. On the other hand, the Internet market is spatial in nature; all marketing stages can happen at the same time.

Time, people, and distribution channels can be disintermediated via the Internet. Companies can move from mass marketing to direct marketing. For example, a manufacturer who has never sold directly to the public may establish an online selling site and provide direct sales by offering partners and consumers direct access to information; thus, the information middleman is eliminated. The presence of fewer steps in the chain of commerce lets the owner of an Internet business engage in more effective direct marketing than the traditional businesses (Haig, 2001; Leebaert, 1998; Sterne, 2001). Grant (1999) indicated that the main reason for this cost saving results is higher profits rather than increased revenues.

In general, companies can become much closer to their consumers by eliminating the middle man and consumers can deal directly with companies without intermediaries. This can certainly increase profitability for companies because the fewer steps of intermediation result in a reduction of the cost of goods sold (Hoffman et al., 1995).

*Distribution Channel*

Another important advantage of Internet commerce to companies is the opportunity to distribute one's products over a far greater area (Hoffman et al., 1995). This is true for both large and small companies. We shall examine the advantages to small companies first.

Small companies benefit because they often have highly specialized products. Having a much larger geographic area is advantageous to small companies, since they can easily saturate the local area with their specialized products and still have inventory on hand (Bunnell & Richard, 2000; Pal & Ray, 2001). The fact is that many e-commerce firms offer highly specialized products that are produced only in a small area, which is an important reason for their appeal. Marcus and Fisher (1986) argued since the beginning of humanity, people have wanted whatever the next tribe on the other side of the hills had – not necessarily because it is better, but simply because it is different. E-commerce sites can often take advantage of this desire for goods and services that cannot be obtained locally.

Large companies that engage in e-commerce benefit from a greater ease of distribution, as well as lower distribution costs. Although larger firms usually have a large-scale distribution system in place before they engage in e-commerce, they still benefit often quite substantially from using e-commerce, because they can reach a worldwide consumer base (Grant, 1999). Obviously, it is one of the fundamentals of business that the more potential consumers one can reach, the more sales one can make. E-commerce allows large companies to reach global consumers (May, 2000).

Generally speaking, Internet tools permit companies to accommodate people who request, and expect, to receive information quickly. In this way, the time to complete business transactions can be reduced. Besides, companies can benefit from the use of the Internet as a distribution channel to reduce traditional distribution expenses and shrink the sale cycle. By using the Internet, buyers and sellers can contact with each other directly, potentially decreasing many labor costs and increase efficiency.

*Gather Information*

From the beginning, the main purpose of companies that employ the Internet is to deliver information about their companies for both internal and external communication. Joyce (2001) illustrated that the trend today is to automate procedures in existing systems. In the automation of procedures, information should be digitized, and can be stored and retrieved via Internet from anywhere in the world. Koehler (1999) described that the Web is the information library; easy to use, easy to update, and universal in its availability. The Internet is the driver of the knowledge economy, and is a natural vehicle for business. Stallings (2001) advocated the importance of information to business as: "A business survives and thrives on information; information within the organization and information exchanged with suppliers, customers, and regulators." (p.131). Suppliers, retailers, and distributors can all benefit from the exchange of information faster and cheaper via the Internet.

Companies also can use Internet technology to gather useful consumers information (Bishop, 1998; Houser, 2001; Rutter & Southerton, 2000). The simplicity of the

Interface between buyer and seller in the virtual world allows a business owner to know very quickly which products or services are the most popular, and given the ease of feedback allowed in e-commerce, can also determine why certain products were or were not popular.

A shopper in a brick-and-mortar store would, in most likelihood, be reluctant to criticize a certain product; they would simply not buy it without giving any direct negative feedback. Likewise, they are likely to buy a product that they liked without telling a business owner why. However, within the more impersonal milieu of a website, people are more likely to provide honest opinions that can help the business owner adjust her or his inventory (Plant, 2000). Bishop (1998) suggested that constantly keep gathering information about consumers and putting consumers' information into a database can facilitate the company fostering more high-quality one-to-one relationship with its consumers.

In general, Internet commerce is networked, which makes it capable of instant updating, storage, retrieval, distribution and sharing of information. The Internet also has the ability to combine many media together, such as radio, television, print, and telephone (Stewart & Zhao, 2000). Companies that embrace Internet technology have an advantage, due to access to information on products, materials, and new ideas in the status quo of industry. The information retrieval and utilization really provide the most important benefit to business usage of the Internet.

*Global Market*

Harrison-Walker (2002) stated that the biggest opportunity for businesses is the ability to reach out to a global audience. Bill Gates stated that the electronic commerce will be enlarged because the usage of personal computer is growing rapidly (Joyce, 2001). Strauss and Fost (2001) estimated that 70% of today's Internet users are based in the U.S.; however, forecasters predicted that 46% Internet users will be based outside the U.S. in 2003. Using Internet, companies can be less concerned with national boundaries, distance, and time zones, because Internet commerce provides a person with the ability to access virtual shopping mall wherever he or she is located.

The advantages of easy access and lower cost of Internet commerce will encourage more small businesses and large traditional firms to enter the global market (Grant, 1999). Union in Geneva estimated that in 1999, just about 2.5% percent of the worldwide population could access the Internet; thus, the Internet still has a huge potential to attract more users and firms to the global village together in the future (Kalin, 1999).

Generally speaking, the advent of Internet commerce has impacted both companies and consumers. For consumers, new media provides the potential to access information from a range of national and international companies. On the other hand, companies can cost-effectively reach more global consumers in the borderless virtual market (Heuberger, 2001; Leebaert, 1998).

*Consumer Support*

The Internet is available 24 hours a day, seven days a week, and 365 days a year. This interactive nature of the medium can be an excellent opportunity to develop deeper and long-term consumer relationships (Newell. 2000; Sindell, 2000; Sterne, 2001). Companies can use the Internet as a communication channel that provides quick support and better service to consumers. For example, a merchant can automatically e-mail electronic newsletters to potential consumers with relevant and useful information. This can keep the relationship between companies and consumers alive for the long term. The companies also can benefit from saving multimillion dollar budgets to maintain consumer relationship through traditional operational tasks (i.e., labor cost, telephone fees, and postage).

The Internet also leads the market to create a one-to-one relationship; every consumer can be seen as a unique person who needs individual focus (Newell, 2000; Plant, 2000; Sindell, 2000). Companies can know individuals better by tracing consumer activities through customers' revealed preferences in navigational purchasing preferences and buying pattern (Leebaert, 1998).

Generally speaking, the Internet allows companies to capture more relevant information from consumers that lets them serve customers more effectively in the future. In the other words, companies can clearly understand each consumer's likes and dislikes, because of the database of consumer information.

*Work Environment*

A final important advantage of e-commerce to the business owner is a low-stress environment in which to work, allowing business owners to balance work, personal life and family. One of the primary reasons that people start their own companies, as well as seek to rise to an executive level in large firms, is that they wish to have a greater measure of control over their workdays. MacKenzie (1997) anticipated the ways in which e-commerce would prove beneficial to business people when he wrote about the beginnings of restructurings of the traditional workplace with the rise of computer technologies. Just as a consumer can shop online at any hour of the day, an e-commerce owner can work at any hour of the day. Upgrading a website, meeting with a new supplier, or shipping orders can be done whenever a business-owner has the time, or inclination to do so.

In addition, the Internet opens new approaches and opportunities for work economics. The University of Texas/Cisco report estimated that the average growth rate of Internet in U.S. is over 175% in 1997 and the revenue is at $301 billion in 1998. The Internet commerce also created 1.2 million jobs opportunity in 1998. The survey also pointed out companies with Internet workers could produce revenue up to 65% higher than other industries (Grant, 1999).

Nowadays, the Internet is a very useful marketing communication medium, which has become a central of life for companies. The Internet offers companies communicate with outside and inside of companies by using networks and can provide rich information that companies can achieve in fulfilling their job function. The Internet could allow companies to sell effectively at a very low cost because the saving of business time and costs (Rutter & Southerton, 2000).

In general, the Internet provides many advantages to companies, such as, fast access to global markets, speedy access to information necessary for decision making, eliminating the middleman through direct marketing, shortened sales cycle, and better consumer support. This lower cost of products or services is based upon decreased overhead for the company, primarily since the fee to maintain a website is far lower than rent or mortgage on a physical property. Additionally, the lower cost of e-commerce also derives from the fact that e-commerce often allows a businessman to cut out some of the many intermediary steps that usually exist between producer and consumer (Microsoft.com, 2003).

### *The Challenge to Companies Using Internet Commerce*

Companies would not venture online in the numbers that they have, and commit such a high percentage of their resources to virtual business, if there were not important benefits to such a business strategy. Marketing is not easy, either in traditional commerce or in e-commerce. Despite the aforementioned benefits to companies with using the Internet, we must now make a counterclaim about e-commerce: There are severe challenges for companies doing virtual business. And the most important challenge is the difference between running or managing a traditional business, and running a virtual one, comes in the arena of marketing the product or services that company offers (Plant, 2000; Reiss, 2000; Robbison et al., 2000).

Marketing forces may now well be the primary force behind a new product. In large corporations, the marketing functions precede the manufacture of a product. Companies come up with an idea, conduct "market" research on the idea to determine if there might be people willing to pay for such a product. Only after they determine this to be the case, does the product itself actually appear. Marketing now often occupies a substantial amount of a firm's time and money, as it has come to include all of the researching and development of new products (Grant Thornron.com, 2003). For an e-commerce firm, marketing is an even more important function than it is for a traditional business, because e-commerce companies are invisible to their consumers without a powerful marketing strategy that includes, at its core, a well-designed website that uses powerful rhetorical tools to recruit and maintains consumers.

Taking advantage of the Internet to bring in new business involves the challenges of developing new strategies and new business process design. An e-commerce strategy centered on a well-designed website can offer many opportunities to a business. However, it can also offer a number of significant challenges, especially to a businessperson who is accustomed to a traditional bricks-and-mortar framework.

*A Web Presence*

Many of the greatest challenges to the owner of an e-commerce firm arise in the area of marketing as the business owners try to determine via virtual distance the needs and desires of their consumers, as well as educating them about the availability of a company's products and the specific features of those goods (May, 2000).

It is in the area of marketing in which some of the greatest challenges arise for the owner or manager of any e-commerce firm. Traditional stores have actual physical structures into which people can walk to look at the merchandise (Plant, 2000). The owners of bricks-and-mortar stores can entice people to come into their stores by brightly lettered signs in the windows. Those same consumers often go into stores with little effort expended on their part. For example, people know to look for furniture sales at certain times of the year and for car sales at others, because these events have occurred for decades. Even without special marketing efforts, a bookstore in a mall can draw consumers in by placing lots of bright and shiny bestsellers in its window casements.

The e-commerce owner has no such traditions and few of these same mechanisms to draw on in marketing his or her company's goods or services. The e-commerce owner also lacks the physical embodiment of the company's goods that the traditional store provides. Grant (1999) asserted that as the Internet becomes more "main trend", every company must address the issue of whether or not it should have an Internet presence. In fact, many traditional brick-and-mortars have been moving into the Internet commerce recently. In the case of a blended business, a business owner may well indeed have a traditional store to work out of along with his or her company's Internet facilities. Such a blended business combines both the virtues along with the drawbacks of both e-commerce and traditional commerce (Stewart & Zhao, 2000; Drapkin, Lowy & Marovitz, 2001). Thus, the e-commerce store owner may spend a great deal of time developing strategies to persuade consumers to buy the company's product. This is why, at least until the high-tech stocks began to crash several years ago, the mantra of the dotcom world has been "market share, market share, market share", which is another way of saying that the e-business owner has to fight nearly constantly to get her or his company's name in front of the public (Plant, 2000).

No product or service is so good that it sells itself. People still have to be informed that it is out there to be bought. A company still has to offer good products along with professional and friendly service. If the company is an e-commerce firm, it also has to have an effective website (Drapkin et al., 2001; Smith, 2000).

In addition to the very basic problem of how one website out of the thousands that now exist can attract consumers is the challenge of satisfying the needs of consumers through websites. Even as business owners are making a shift from an orientation developed in the traditional business milieu to one that works in the virtual world, customers are also making this same shift (Leebaret, 1998). Because the commercial world is in a transitional phase right now, the expectations of consumers are a mixture of what they once expected of stores, and what they are just learning to expect from websites and e-commerce (Hill, 2002).

With consumers both expecting e-commerce to act like traditional businesses but also virtual businesses, it is often a distinct challenge for the e-commerce owner to meet both sets of expectations, keep his or her consumers happy, and instill in them a sense of loyalty. This challenge may fade in time as consumers become increasingly familiar with the norms of e-commerce and as those norms themselves become increasingly solidified (Giddens, 2000).

*Competition*

The Internet is providing both opportunities and challenges to marketers. Due to the borderless marketplace and unlimited time nature of Internet commerce, it is much easier for consumers to shop and buy on the Internet than on foot. Consumers can check product information and prices by visiting different websites in a few minutes. Because this reason, the competition in the new economy should be sharper than in the old economy (Haig, 2001).

Moreover, small companies are able to access a global market, too. No matter how big or small, companies have the same ease of access to potential consumers (Grant, 1999; Isidro, 2002; Pal & Ray, 2001; Plant, 2000). While the lines between traditional (i.e. brick-and-mortar) businesses were fairly clear-cut at the beginning of the Internet revolution, they have been getting fuzzier and fuzzier ever since. It is now possible for a one-person, highly specialized company to use the Internet to break down many of the marketing and distribution barriers that for years have limited small companies. It means the Internet has broken the conventional view that only the biggest companies can win the battle in globalizing economy. Pal and Ray (2001) pointed out the earlier marketing rules such as: "companies are either number one, or they are nobody" is no longer true; actually, the global market can be shared among many competitors via Internet.

Many researchers (Colby, 2002; Grant, 1999; Sterne, 2001; Terry, 1999) indicated that with a skilled use of the Internet, a small company can have global consumers – just as a multinational company reaches around the world to find its customers. Indeed, the Internet has emerged with strategic importance for all small and medium-sized enterprises (SMEs) in electronic commerce. Carroll and Broadhead (2001) explained that a small company's flexible, innovative management style could provide a competitive ability in the highly dynamic Internet environment. Obviously, small companies can have the ability to challenged established companies that had well-known identification by taking the advantage of new medium.

A Forrester Research report showed that e-business could rise five times every two or three years, and it will reach $6.8 trillion worldwide by 2004 (Pal & Ray, 2001). A 2000 study by International Communications Research found that marketing and e-commerce are currently the top features of the Web that small businesses participate in the most (Albee Cibops Smart Web business.com, 2001). Table 3 shows the different features of small business use of the Internet in 1999.

The report by Albee Cibops Smart Web business.com (2002) illustrated that small businesses (fewer than 100 employees) comprise approximately 98% of all firms in the U.S. The huge number of small business will have a significant impact on the Web market. Table 4 shows that almost every small business in US. is becoming, or will be soon, connected to the Internet.

Table 3

*The Different Features of Small Business Use of the Internet in 1999 (Albee Cibops Smart Web business.com, 2002).*

| Promoting to Prospects | -------------------- 69% |
|---|---|
| E-Commerce | ---------------- 57% |
| Improving Customer Service | ---------- 48% |
| Competing with other Firms | ---------- 46% |
| Communicating with Employees | -- 11% |

Table 4

*Number of U.S. Small Businesses Connected to the Internet from 1999 to 2002 (Albee Cibops Smart Web business.com, 2002).*

| 1999 | 2,996,280 | 41% |
|---|---|---|
| 2000 | 4,461,534 | 60% |
| 2001 | 5,895,694 | 79% |
| 2002 | 6,300,306 | 80% |

Compared to other traditional distribution methods, the cost of setting up a Web online shopping is very low. According to Association of National Advertisers 1998, they estimated that the average cost of building a website is $ 228,000, and the maintaining fee of the site is $ 150,000 (Stewart & Zhao, 2000). As might be expected, the low cost of producing a website could create intensified competition for many marketing organizations (Rutter & Southerton, 2000).

Hall (2001) stated that the interactive nature of the Internet environment allows consumers to actively deep search what they really want. It is very obviously that consumers will dominate the World Wide Wed Marketing strategy. For instance, usually, the price marked in stores is an asking price, not the best price. However, consumers can employ comparative shopping searches to find the cheapest products price among different websites without a trouble. The Internet increases the bargaining power of consumers; consumers have the ability to know quickly if there is a difference in price between two dealers. Rutter and Southerton (2000) stated that, "Not only will consumers be presented with greater choice but, because of the increase of competition between retailers, the price of those products should be driven down." (p. 144). Under above-mentioned situation, the competition in the Internet commerce is much intense than the traditional commerce.

In summary, the Internet truly creates a more facilitating environment that confers a benefit for global participation. However, these lower start-up costs have decreased barriers to entry in Internet commerce, which has created more trade competitors worldwide. Companies need to have appropriate strategies to deal with the fierce competition in the Web-based marketing. One of the important ways is to create a high-quality website that can promote consumer satisfaction to reduce "click-away rates", and then facilitate the completion of online purchases or repeat purchase behaviors.

### The Benefits and Challenges to Consumers Using Internet Commerce
#### *The Benefits to Consumers Using Internet Commerce*

The benefits to consumers who use e-commerce are in many ways the obverse of those that accrue to the business owner. This is certainly true in traditional commerce as well as in virtual commerce, and it should not in fact surprise us, since the goals of the customer and that of the business owner are in many ways congruent to each other: Both want the best deal possible of out every exchange. Of course, consumers want to maximize their savings while business-owners want to maximize their profits, but both want to feel that they have been treated fairly and gotten the best deal. At the end of every commercial transaction (whether virtual or real-world), ideally both sides will look forward to doing business together again.

Van Duyne, Landay and Hong (2002) advocated that the Internet is increasingly integrated into consumers' lives. Obviously, the Internet is providing consumers the ability to access a wider range of goods and services, potentially at cheaper prices across borders. It also made it possible to trade beyond traditional trading hours. Indeed, buying on the Internet opens a whole new range of possibilities; anyone with access to a computer that has an Internet connection can buy almost anything from anywhere around the world. From the consumers' perspective, electronic commerce provides significant benefits when compared with traditional shopping.

This book categorizes consumers' benefits using Internet from four different perspectives, such as convenience, lower price, greater selection, and more complete information.

*Convenience*

The online shopping provides an attractive alternative to traditional shopping practices. Consumers can make purchases from their comfort home or work environment, 24 hours a day, 7 days a week. Online consumers can shop products and services around the world at the speed of light (Bishop, 1998). Some consumer behavior scholars define the convenience of online shopping as saving time and effort, including physical and mental effort (Wolfinbarger & Gilly, 2001). We can say the major benefit to consumers is that the Internet gives shoppers plenty of convenience (Jarvenpaa & Todd, 1996; Rutter & Southerton, 2000). People do not need to conform to the social conventions of grooming anymore if they like to shop at three a.m. in their pajamas. For them, the Internet is fundamentally appealing.

Wolfinbarger and Gilly (2001) found that many online buyers also enjoy the feeling of freedom, control, the lack of sociality, and anonymity:

> Absent online are salespeople, spouse, crowds, and lines. Moreover, the ability to find what they need and to completely a transaction without having to go through a human being is associated by online buyers with increased freedom and control. An additional benefit of people being absent online is anonymity; some online buyers visit upscale sites or stores where they might be embarrassed to shop offline. (Wolfinbarger & Gilly, 2001, p.40).

Consumers can purchase all around the world with "one click"– no more standing in line, no more hassles. Van Duyne et al. (2002) identified that convenience in the shopping process means that it requires minimum efforts and assures time saving. In short, as the Internet becomes an integral part of our lives, online websites will attract consumers by convenience, and the value of time, as well.

*Lower Price*

As e-business owners have the advantage of being able to cut costs and so undercut the prices of their bricks-and-mortar competitors, low prices are also an advantage to e-commerce consumers (Strauss & Forst, 2001). Many e-retailers keep their costs as low as possible, in order to provide strong incentives for attracting their consumers (Wolak, 2000). Moreover, the lower price derives from reducing intermediary transaction, because consumers can order the product directly from merchants (Wigand & Benjamin, 1995).

Undeniably, the Internet puts comparison shopping at a consumer's fingertips, due to the interactive and networked nature of the Internet. It is easier to engage the price comparison shopping on the Web than in traditional stores. With the help of search engines, price comparisons of multiple sellers can be conducted at once. Consumers become more informed and have more alternatives to consider before making their final decision. The lower price becomes a reason for many consumers choose to shop online (Stern, 2001).

*Greater Selection*

The Internet brings dramatic improvements to economic efficiency. Consumers benefit from the convenience of online purchasing from the growing variety of products sold on the Web. There is also a huge potential for locating hard-to-find products when the local offline store is out of stock (Hoffman et al., 1995). For example, Amazon.com has the ability to offer millions of books to their consumers, including some books which are out of print. On the other hand, the typical retail bookstore usually stocks no more than 25,000 books at a point of time. In the virtual store, e-retailers can offer some slow moving items or particular inventories, at lower cost than traditional retailing.

May (2000) mentioned that, "E-commerce firms have to charge the shipping cost of their products. They do so either by charging upfront shipping costs or by embedding the costs of shipping in the costs of their products." (p.119). Although the shipping costs could undercut to some extent the savings that they make in their businesses, such a disadvantage can be minimized by companies that offer products which cannot be bought in any bricks-or-mortar store nearby.

Generally speaking, online shopping allows consumers acquire products that are not available locally, and pay less than they did in traditional stores. Ultimately, consumers who have the specific products they desire to buy will see the Internet as an ideal place to find greater selection.

*More Information*

Providing sufficient information is an important benefit to consumers via Internet (Bishop, 1998; Carliner, 2002; Leebaert, 1998; Plant, 2000; Sterne, 2001). The Internet is increasing access to information and much of that information is free. Consider this: With the worldwide million computers connected to the Internet, the amount of information is extremely surprising. Harrison-Walker (2002) affirmed that, "the buying process begins with problem recognition and identification of alternatives" (p.19). Many consumers like to use the Internet as a resource of product information before they buy.

The Internet offers consumers the benefit of 24 hours and 7 days a week to access various amounts of information for consumer decision-making (Carliner, 2002; Hoffman et al., 1995; Mann, 2002). Consumers can easily gather information without going out to several stores searching. For Instance, consumers can enter a consumer service website, and search for the FAQ (Frequently Asked Questions) page to know the specific questions' suggestions and solutions, instead of using telephone. Thus, the hours of telephone time and fees can be saved.

The recent study by Wolfinbarger and Gilly (2001) advocated that many online consumers believe that they can find more useful and clear information without the help of salesman in offline store. For example, Smarter Kids. com provides a function on Web for consumer who want find a matching toy for child by typing the child's age and learning goal into the ActiveBuyersGuide. The computer can find the matching toy for the child.  Berry (2003) described that an online support center can empower consumers to help themselves quickly and effectively.  By allowing consumers to be autonomous in seeking solutions, companies can keep their consumers satisfied and establish good relationships, while reducing support costs.

In short, consumers can access a worldwide market of suppliers who offer a huge choice and variety of information for goods and services.  As a result, the Internet can be viewed as a utilitarian activity to consumers, because the search costs are reduced than traditional stores.

*Better Service*

Online shopping is growing in popularity.  One reason for online shopping's rise so rapidly is because the Internet is associated with the convenience of overnight delivery and service (Strauss & Forst, 2001).  Consumer service over the Web is likely to be more reliable, and can provide consistent service, than traditional retailing (Stern, 1997).  For instance, with e-mail, service does not need to stop at the end of the day.  E-mail response allows companies to maintain an ongoing dialogue with consumers, to ensure they are satisfied with their purchase.  Sterne (2001) revealed that superb service can create happy consumers, repeat customers, and world-of-mouth referrals.  In fact, outstanding consumer service is one of the most important factors that can affect consumers' retention (Dugan, 2000; Sindell, 2000).  In short, websites can allow dot.com sellers provide more detailed, specific information and a trustworthy attitude to their consumers than traditional retail store.

## *The Challenge to Consumers Using Internet Commerce*
*No Security and Privacy*

Just as the benefits of e-commerce for the business owner are matched by a number of challenges, the benefits of e-commerce for the consumer are also matched by challenges that the consumer is faced with.  Primary among these is the lack of security and privacy that many consumers feel in buying on-line.  A 2002 survey by Forrester research showed that only 21.2 percent consumers believed their personal data was secure when they shopped online (ePaynews.com, 2002). In other words, consumers perceive risk when they purchase online.

As the Internet grows and the electronic flow of information increases, more and more concerns will be raised regarding the security of documents, e-mails and information. Consumers may be concern about the security of providing personal information, or making payment online, because of the difficulties in assessing the difference between a legitimate company and a deceptive one. Stallings (2000) declared that although the Internet is very good at its broad distribution, which also makes it a dangerous place to do business. There is a high probability that consumers' confidential information (e.g., credit card number and personal information) may be abused or sold to third party by the vendor in the Internet environment.

In traditional commerce contexts, a consumer's trust can be found in a physical building or salesman; thus, the large traditional bricks-and-mortar can take the advantage in the Internet market if it chooses a Web presence (Geyskens, Steenkamp, Scheer, & Kumar, 1996; Grant, 1999; Peeples, 2002). Consumers recognize their brand and know there is a real business behind the website. This kind of assurance can increase consumers' affirmative feeling with a website. On the other hand, the pure Web-based company, such as Amazon.com, thus faces a situation in which consumer trust could be inherently low. Some consumers desire careful online shopping information, because it helps guarantee that the company is legitimate. Retailers on the Internet need to develop excellent long-term consumer relationship to establish and earn consumers' trust through relevant activities on the websites (Peeples, 2002).

Given the absence of physical exposure and contact, it is very difficult to identify whether company is reputable on the Internet. To ensure the continued growth of e-commerce, companies should think securing consumers as a worthy investment, and take more care in storing consumers' personal information today.

*Lack of Touch Feeling*

In an online shopping environment, another disadvantage to the consumer is the difficulty in verifying the quality of goods without examining them directly (Braddock, 2001; Colby, 2002; May, 2001). Winn and Beck (2002) indicated that there is no

61

physical interaction between the consumer and the product. Usually, consumers want to actually see, feel, smell or taste, before they make buying decision. For example, a dress might look good on a website, but a lot of consumers would want to touch it to see how soft the fabric is. A jar of guava jelly might look sumptuous, but there is no way for an online consumer to get a taste of the product before hand. The touch and feel sensory still remain in shoppers' expectations. Thus, some consumers may still prefer the personal shopping experience, which as Armstrong called it "retail recovery" (Colby, 2002).

In the virtual stores, consumers can only make decisions based on the information that websites provided; thus, the question is whether the website design can help consumers overcome the barriers of "no-touch feeling" should be a very important issue to a successful online business. The study by Wolfinbarger and Gilly (2001) found that some consumers will check out items off-line before they buy online to overcome with the inability to touch. In short, it is important for e-commerce sites to compensate the sensory information to consumers in a certain dimension, in order to balance the lack of physical feeling in the virtual store (Stewart & Zhao, 2000; Winn & Beck, 2002).

## The Important Role of Website Design in Internet Commerce
### *Overview*

The Internet has been bringing a fundamental change to human life. Many of the things we do in our daily life can be done now on the Internet. For example, we can play games, shop, do research, and learn, etc. The Internet can combine various media, such as text, graphics, sound, and video to present information. Moreover, the Internet is not only a communication medium, but also a business medium. Carroll and Brodhead (2001) explained that in traditional media, the medium is the message; however, in the World Wide Web, the medium is the marketplace. In fact, the amount of consumers shopping and purchasing online has rise dramatically. The study by Bulkeley and Carlton (2000) estimated that there are over 30,000 online businesses selling directly to consumers. Commerce Net (2001) report showed in January 2000, the Internet had already connected 242 million users worldwide; as of August 2001, the number of online population was

513.41 million. That means Business-to-Consumer (B2C) e-commerce faces more and more potential consumers globally.

Certainly, compared to other traditional distribution methods, to set up a website is very easy and the cost is low. However, after a company enters the Internet market, it really requires many considerable thoughts to support its business. There is a risk involved in building a website because, while simple to build, a website does not guarantee to facilitate sales (Harrison-Walker, 2002).

There are lots of reasons that can lead to consumers' resistance when purchasing online. It is very important to create an effective Web design in a rapidly changing electronic environment, because consumers will not take a second look at an ineffective designed site (Newell, 2000; Sterne, 2001). Many reports have shown that online businesses are "all hype and no profit" (Quick, 2000). A company needs to understand that choosing to launch a website should both reinforce business future, and open up extra economic opportunities. Indeed, websites are excellent business tools that can extent companies' marketing, sales, and consumer relationship management (Cai, 2001; Creativeflavor.com, 2003).

Launching a site with a deficient design may waste money since it will not attract and retain consumers. Besides, websites are the main contact with public; a poorly-designed website can seriously damage the reputation of companies (Steehouder & Coney, 2000). In order to succeed, companies need to learn from both the victories, and mistakes, of others from e-commerce history. It is very important that marketers can follow some critical website design rules when they spending time and money on building websites. Companies have to understand that the look and feel of an e-commerce website must fully consistent with consumers' needs. However, the trouble with many websites is that designers think from a technical perspective, not from the consumer's perspective. Undoubtedly, websites should have the effective ability to attract consumers and persuade them to buy. In this book, the researcher suggested that when designing a website, a rhetoric perspective approach can improve more effective to consumers than a purely technological perspective. The intention of this book was to show how to design a persuasive website through theories and methods pertaining to visual persuasion.

*Previous Researches on Website Design*

As electronic commerce continues to grow throughout the world, the demands for greater knowledge about how to design a highly persuasive website on the new electronic based Internet marketing continue to increase. Many recent studies and books have been initiated as "how-to manuals"; they are step-by-step guides to creating a website business presence (e.g., Fry & Paul, 1995; Shafer & Smith, 1997; Zimmaner, 2001). They tried to show readers how to follow guidelines to launch a website in a short time. Unfortunately, little time was spent on preparing people to create a high-quality website.

Some research studies focused on the technological aspect of website design. Those studies addressed strengths and weaknesses of Web page design software for new technologies to solve current problems (e.g., Baumgardt, 2002; Bell & Castagna, 1997; Foster, Emberton & Bauer, 2001; Page, 2002; Reinhardt & Lott, 2002). These articles or books focused on teaching readers how to use different Web software such as: Flash, Photoshop, and Dreamwaver to establish a website successfully; however, this may result in a low-quality website, if readers do not fully understand some theoretical background before they create a website. Likewise, many others presented website design guidelines based almost entirely on the opinions of experts (e.g., Coney & Steehouder, 2000; D. K., Frakas & J. B., Franks, 2000; Greenberg, 1998; Houser, 2001; Johnson-Sheehan & Baehr, 2001; Patrick & Lynch, 1997; Williams, 2000) rather than on the results of empirical research. Topics explored by these authors include use of screen color, choice of font, space, and size for textual material, design of a grid, and other user interface issues. These earlier studies did demystify some certain factors that drive the success of e-commerce website. Little research, however, directly addresses the issue of the persuasive power of influencing online consumers' experience to visit, purchase, and loyalty.

The fact is that there is not a comprehensive established theory in the area of persuasive websites design available presently in the e-commerce context to date. However, several researchers (e.g., Hampton, 1990; Keivn, 1996; Jarvenpaa & Todd, 1996; Liu & Arnett 2000; Winn & Beck 2002) in the past have followed similar research approaches. For example, Hampton (1990) linked the rhetoric's persuasive characteristics to visual design. He argued that we need to take a new approach to technology world – a visual perspective. Hampton explained the way to incorporate rhetorical function to the visual schema in his study. However, his research was limited to noncommercial contexts.

Keivn (1996) presented a framework grounded in the rhetorical concept of ethos. He encouraged organizations to establish sites with trustworthy content. Keivn (1996) stated that an ethos site required more spatial orientation than print documents, but Keivn did not directly address which ethos factors could affect the credibility of websites and he did not investigate the three rhetorical elements (i.e., logos, ethos and pathos) together.

Jarvenpaa and Todd (1996) derived three main groups of factors that affect consumers' shopping attitude, such as product perceptions (price, variety, product quality), shopping experience (effort, compatibility, playfulness), and customer service (responsiveness, reliability, tangibility, empathy). These researchers derived their results from a small sample open-ended survey, and there were no clear explanations why these factors are important for consumer loyalty.

Liu and Arnett (2000) indicated four factors that are important to website success in e-commerce, such as information and service quality, system use, playfulness, and system design quality. Their results were from observing different websites practices; however, not from a systematic analysis.

Winn and Beck (2002) listed logos (price, variety, product information, effort), pathos (playfulness, tangibility, empathy), and ethos (recognizability, compatibility, assurance, reliability) as the real value of websites. They attempted to make the salient factors of Jarvenpaa and Todd (1996) more narrow and applicable in order to measure design elements on e-commerce websites. Although Winn and Beck's study was the first research that incorporated all three rhetorical elements and applied them to commercial website design, they did not investigate whether these rhetorical factors can truly influence the revenue of e-commerce websites.

The current literature does not reveal the comprehensive answers about the important design factors as influences on the Business-to-Consumer (B2C) e-commerce websites. However, these earlier studies of Internet shopping provide a useful point of departure for current research. The purpose of this research was to investigate empirically-based principles that Web designers can employ to improve the likelihood that consumers will happily visit, and become loyal to a site. The outcomes of the research are likely to be significance to Internet commerce, consumers, and researchers.

### Aristotle's Rhetorical Theory

Rhetoric was written between 360 and 334 B.C by Aristotle, who is also known as the father of logic. Aristotle was a Greek philosopher, educator, and scientist. He combined the ideas of earlier philosophers such as Socrates and Plato, and then created his own thoughts of rhetoric. Aristotle defined rhetoric as "the ability, in each particular case, to see three available means of persuasion" (Kennedy, 1991, p.36-37). Roberts (2000) defined rhetoric as: "the faculty of observing in any given case the available means of persuasion." (p. 2). In fact, one of the most distinguished aspects of Aristotle was the concept of pisteis, or proofs. Aristotle believed that there were three means of persuasion about the art of public speaking, such as logos, pathos, and ethos (Lamb, 1998).

Kennedy (1991) explained these three things as below:

> First, the truth and logical validity of what being argued; second, the speaker's success in conveying to the audience the perception that he or she can be trusted; and third, the emotions that a speaker is able to awaken in an audience to accept the views advanced and act in accordance with them (Kennedy, 1991, p.5).

Covino and Jolliffe (1995) mentioned that Aristotle believed that, "the function of rhetoric is not to persuade but to see the available means of persuasion in each case" (p.3). Clearly speaking, the three means of persuasion are dependent on (1) to reason logically, (2) to understand human character and goodness in their various forms, and (3) to understand the emotions (Roberts, 2001). Basically, these three means of persuasion are all intertwined although they completely different (Kenndy, 1991).

### Three Cornerstones of Persuasion

Dormann (1997) explained that, "rhetoric originated from the functional organization of verbal discourse, and its object is eloquence (or proficiency) defined as effective speech designed to influence and to convince others." (p.345). The rhetorical theory includes three modes of appeal: logos, pathos, and ethos.

66

*Logos*

Logos can be translated into "reason". In rhetoric, logos is the rational and logical proofs. Logos is one of the many things that a speaker needs to consider in order to form a logical argument. Aristotle believed logos as thought manifested in speech. In general, logos can be the first thought that comes to our mind when we think about persuasion. The speaker must provide logical reasons to support their claims, in order to persuade their audiences (Covino & Jolliffe, 1995).

*Pathos*

Pathos can be translated into "pathetic" or emotional proofs. Pathos stimulates the feelings of the audience, and tries to change their attitudes and actions (Covino & Jolliffe, 1995). Kennedy (1991) indicated that, "Emotions should be considered in terms of what the state of mind is the person who feels particular emotion, in regard to whom the emotion is felt, and for what reason." (p.17). Roberts (2000) advocated that, "Persuasion may come through the hearers, when the speech stirs their emotions." (p.3). Generally speaking, pathos is one of three forms of persuasion in rhetoric; however, pathos is closely related with ethos and logos. For example, it is more likely to have an effect in one's speech if the logical reasons can fit the emotional proofs of audiences. Although many people think that the logical thoughts are the main factors to influence our decision making, Aristotle affirmed that emotions can greatly influence our judgments (Howard, 1997).

*Ethos*

Aristotle defined ethos as the credibility that the speaker established (Kennedy, 1991). Ethos moves an audience by proving the credibility of the orator, and eventually achieves the main purpose of the speech – to persuade. Hovland, Janis and Kelly (1953) explained that audiences are more likely to believe the speaker is credible if they can perceive practical wisdom, integrity, trustworthiness, and goodwill. Conversely, audiences will not feel confident about a speaker if they feel untrustworthiness and dishonesty in personality or character.

## The Keys to Successful Web Design: A Rhetorical Approach

Online shopping malls appear to be one of the most attractive and fastest growing areas of businesses. However, many websites designs are too unattractive to capture consumers' attention and sell goods. A study by Braddock (2000) showed that only 0.04 percent of all websites have 80 percent of all consumer visits. It means to design websites; companies really need to combine theoretical and practical strategies that can attract the largest consumers as possible. Winn and Beck (2002) stated that classic rhetoric is a good strategy that companies can adopt to persuade consumers to visit, and stay with, the site. Laffoon (1998) declared that, "rhetoric is a design knowledge...that is cohesive and problem focused." (p.90). Indeed, rhetorical strategy is a good choice to persuade people by rational, emotional, and credibility since design is the method to use logical and aesthetic modes to influence others in both emotional and logical way (Ehse, 1989).

Coney and Steehouder (2000) emphasized that, "When the rhetorical principle is applied to Web design, it provides powerful insights and strategies for designing and evaluating online communication." (p.327). From the view of communication, Web designers are keeping engaged in active dialog with consumers. Companies need to have effectively persuasive power to win consumers' heart. Winn and Beck (2002) described that the applications of rhetorical theory in websites as:

> Classical rhetoric provides a theoretical framework for understanding the interaction between the customer and the interface design. Indeed, e-commerce sites and design elements from which they are built serve a classic rhetorical function: they are a means of persuading potential customers to explore the content on commercial sites, to interact with the site, and ultimately to reach the act of purchasing (Winn & Beck, 2002, p.19).

Generally speaking, rhetoric is a very important ability that needs to be cultivated in communication areas today (Lamb, 1998). The aim of persuasive Web designs are to change users by motives them to think, feel, or act differently. To do that, a website needs to offer consumers with reasons that can convince them to purchase. An effective website design is not something the website "does to" consumers. It is an engagement between a website and consumers (Cato, 2001). Websites need to have the rhetorical ability – to persuade their consumers by logos, pathos, and ethos.

### The Power of Persuasion in Marketing

Taillard (2000) stated that there are two major goals of human communication: to be understood, and to be believed. He described persuasion as: "We try to affect our audiences' beliefs, desires and action. Persuasion is the communicative act that carries out both these goals – an audience that has been persuaded has understood an utterance, and believed its message." (p.1). Mortensen (2003) illustrated persuasion as one of the oldest arts of humankind. Persuasion is to motivate and influence, not force people to do what you want. Aristotle believed that persuasion relies on artistic, not inartistic proofs (Covino & Jolliffe, 1995). Since rhetoric is one of the effective skills of communication, its theory can be applied to many facets in different areas such as: graphic design (e.g., Ehses, 1989), advertising (e.g., McQuairrie & Mick, 1996; Scott, 1994), writing (e.g., Troffer, 2000), and films (e.g., Whitock, 1990). As a result, these previous studies can guide the future research in website design.

A recent study carried out by Recker and Kathman (2001) indicated that, "The relationship among design, marketing, and consumer behavior has their roots firmly established in both psychology and physiology." (p.70). In fact, part of the process of selling, whether on-line, or in-person is the art of persuading a consumer that he or she will benefit from buying a specific product from a particular company. Most products that an individual buys are not a question of life or death, and most products can be bought from more than one place. Therefore, if a company wants to be successful in selling their products to a customer, that company must both offer a good product and good service, as well as a talent for persuasion (Schiffman & Kanuk, 1994). It would be a mistake to dismiss the importance of the power of persuasion in our current culture, and in the way in which the market is currently constructed. Indeed, the power of persuasion is of extraordinary and critical importance. A significant percentage of sales cannot be made only from the strength of the product itself, or of any promise of service, but also because of the power of persuasion (Mortensen, 2003).

A well-designed website can help close a sale, can help persuade a consumer that this is the place and this is the time to buy (May, 2000). Mortensen (2003) affirmed that in many ways, the website is only a more sophisticated version of the print advertising; however, this is not to devalue the design of a website, but rather to link it to ancient human practices of commerce. Commercial transactions lie at the heart of a great deal of human activity, and websites are only the latest manifestation of the ancient human practice of buying, and selling, and persuading others, that what one has to sell is better than the seller in the next village, or the next block, or the next University Resource Locators (URLs) (Terry, 1999).

In summary, in the virtual environment, the central question to marketers is how to make site more persuasive to help their consumers easily make decisions. Novak et al., (1999) argued that consumer experience in online environment is a critical issue to create advantage on the Internet. Many website designs; however, make consumers confused and frustrated in the virtual stores, because many designers have a lack of knowledge about what the consumer desires. If consumers cannot find what they want, or have a bad experience on a website, it is very difficult to persuade him or her to come back again. In other words, website designs that utilize rhetorical strategies, to create a welcoming buying environment, will have better opportunity to discourage the chance of "clicking away".

### Critical Website Design Elements by Winn and Beck

Williamson and Johnson (1995) stated that the main challenges in Internet commerce is attracting consumers to their websites and generating repeat visits. Website designs require strategies, and rhetorical theory provides an effective guiding principle. Since websites are often the main contact with consumers in the Internet market, the visual elements in a company's website may include some persuasive components that have impact on a potential customer's positive experience. It is expected that increased levels of the consumers' positive experience would lead shoppers to have more optimistic attitudes toward websites, stronger purchase intention and loyalty (Sindell, 2000; Smith, 2000). Companies need a detailed understanding about critical website design elements to get their websites' operation up and running, and to make websites durable over the long term.

Winn and Beck (2002) analyzed the importance of an effective website design for an overall e-commerce strategy. They argued that a successful and effective website design does not require an entirely new set of rhetorical rules, but rather relies on established rules of oratory and rhetoric. In other words, the successful website shares a number of attributes with a successful advertisement in a magazine, or a successful speech.

Winn and Beck (2002) carefully developed a way to examine the persuasive power of design elements on an e-commerce website as follows:

*Logos*: There are four sub-variables under logos (price, variety, production information, and effort):

Central to Winn and Beck's analysis is the concept of logos, or the internal logic of the site. This internal logic includes the way the site addresses the issue of price presentation, which is the ease of determining the price of an object, combined with any additional charges such as shipping. Also essential to the logic of a site is the idea of "variety". Winn and Beck define this attribute as the ways in which a website addresses the issue of providing an accurate description of the company's products, by exhibiting the breadth and depth of product variety.

Also central to a good website design, according to Winn and Beck, is a clear and complete presentation of product information. They stated that the most successful websites are those that provide sufficient product detail to help a customer make an informed decision. Winn and Beck also argued that any successful website must minimize the effort that a customer has to expend in buying a product by providing clear, unambiguous, and detailed cues at each step of the process, to allow the customers to orient themselves throughout the process of buying a product.

*Pathos*: Three sub-variables under pathos (playfulness, tangibility, and empathy)

Winn and Beck mentioned that the successful website does not end with logos attributes. They stated that websites should contain an element of "playfulness", so that a customer is not only informed by the site, but also entertained by it. A fun experience can ensure consumers a good time, and encourage them come back again. The successful website should also contain an element of what Winn and Beck referred to as "tangibility", which is the ability of the website design to compensate to the consumer for the absence of sensory input that occurs when a consumer is not in direct contact with a product.

71

Winn and Beck also argued another most important aspect of good website design is the element of empathy. An empathetic attitude on the part of the vendor is an essential part of the process of selling to that person. This was true long before the process of selling and buying became something that one could do from the privacy of one's own home. They believed personalizing the site is the best way to show empathy toward consumers.

*Ethos*: There are four sub-variables under ethos (recognizability, compatibility, assurance, and reliability)

Winn and Beck argued that a successful website is a "credible" one. In other words, an effective website is one that gains people's trust. Such trust is built up through what the two authors call "recognizability", which is equivalent to brand-name recognition and loyalty. A good website also embodies the concept of "compatibility", which is a measure of the extent to which a site encourages consumers to believe that they belong to a community. "Assurance" is also an important quality of the successful website, because it is essential to convince potential consumers that their privacy and security are guaranteed by the company. Finally, Winn and Beck argued that the successful website is one that seems reliable to its consumers. These potential customers must come to have good faith in the business, and trust there will be ease of communication between the consumer and the business. A high-quality consumer service is the best way to build company's reliability.

### *Definitions of Independent Variables*

This research employed Winn and Beck's research taxonomy (2002), which is grounded in classic rhetorical concept of logos, pathos, and ethos. There were thirteen independent variables used in this research. Major independent variables are Age, Gender, Logos, Pathos, and Ethos. The definitions of each independent variable are following:

*Age*: In this research, Age was divided into four groups: 18-22 years, 23-35 years, 36-50 years, and 51 or older.

*Gender*: In this research, gender was divided into two groups: males and females.

*Logos*:

Winn and Beck (2002) declared that logos appeals to logic. Aristotle described logos as thought manifested in speech. It is the logical reason that the audience finds convincing and persuasive (Covino & Jolliffe, 1995). Based on abovementioned descriptions, the researcher defined logos in this research as: Logos is the persuasion of consumers by using logic on websites. Logos is the power of reasoning shared by the site and the consumers.

*Pathos*:

Winn and Beck (2002) declared that pathos appeals to emotions. Aristotle used pathos to refer to the form of persuasion based on emotion. This emotional power can positively effect one's judgments (Covino & Jolliffe, 1995). Based on aforementioned descriptions, the researcher defined pathos in this research as: Pathos is the persuasion of consumers by using emotion on websites. Pathos can stimulate the feelings of consumers, and seeks to change their attitudes and actions toward a site.

*Ethos*:

Winn and Beck (2002) declared that ethos appeal to credibility. Roberts (2000) stated that Aristotle used ethos to refer to the speaker's character as it appears to the audience. Based on abovementioned descriptions, the researcher defined ethos in this research as: the credibility that the website has established. Ethos can persuade consumers by providing the credibility of the site.

Sub- independent Variables:

*Logos*: Four independent variables under logos. They are price, variety, production information, and effort.

1. *Price*:

Available evidence suggests that prices on the Internet are lower than those for comparable goods purchased through other commercial channels. It is the main reason why many consumers choose online shopping (Keeney, 1999). Podlogar (1998) defined price as: "… competitively priced merchandise and attractive promotions and deals." (p.2). Jarvenpaa and Todd (1997) illustrated that price is the total monetary cost for consumers to purchase a good or service, including different transaction costs, such as shipping fees. Winn and Beck (2002) mentioned that designers cannot decide the price for goods or service on the site; however, designers can use price presentation as a rhetorical tool to persuade consumers' price perception.

The researcher defined *Price* in this research as price presentation. Consumers can have positive attitudes toward websites, if the site can provide attractive price options to them, such as: price comparisons with competitors, sales, discounts, and special offers. The goal is to design a price presentation on the website that can support consumers' price-conscious shopping habits, and facilitate consumers making purchase decisions quickly.

2. *Variety*:

Podlogar (1998) defined variety as: "… a wide range of goods and services on the site". (p.2). Winn and Beck (2002) advocated that designers should create the ability for consumers to easily find what they are looking for on the site.

The researcher defined *Variety* in this research as product structure and display on websites. Consumers can have positive feelings with a website, if the site can present an accurate representation of products by exhibiting the breadth and depth of product variety.

3. *Product information*:

Tabor (1999) stated that quality information is the best tool to win consumer acceptance on a website. Carliner (2002) illustrated that providing information is an optimal strategy for companies. He defined the perfect information design as: "Preparing communication products so that they achieve the performance objectives established for them." (p.43). Mountford (1990) mentioned that the biggest challenge to Web designers is how to best present the product information on websites. The major job of information is to provide consumers with quality product knowledge to facilitate their choice and buying decision. People often visit familiar websites many times in one week. Therefore, companies need to ensure that their information is fresh and up-to-date on their website (Haig, 2001; Patrick & Lynch, 1997).

74

The researcher defined *Product Information* in this research as the structure and display of product information on websites. Consumers can have optimistic feelings with a website, if the site can provide very clear, detailed and up-to-date information about products, so as to make consumers' decision-making easier.

4. *Effort*:

Kirkby (2001) stated that ease of use is the most important factor for online shopping. Jarvenpaa and Todd (1996) declared that effort means "saving time and makes shopping easy." (p.66). Many customers know how it feels to be "lost in hyperspace". Andrisani, Gaal, Gillette, and Steward (2001) identified three situations about disorientation on the site: (1) users do not know where to go next, (2) users know where to go but do not know how to get there, and (3) users do not know their current position relative to the overall document structure. Johnson-Sheehan and Baehr (2001) affirmed that designers should visualize the "future paths" that users may have on the site to lessen their effort. Smith (2000) explained the easy navigation as: "two or three clicks to any solution, fast page loads, effective search engines, a quick shopping checkout process, server reliability, ability to handle peak load times and so on." (p.227). Andrisani et al. (2001) also emphasized that it is important for designers to make websites understandable and navigable for their users. websites need to provide enough navigation mechanisms so that users can find their desired information in the fewest steps (Lynch & Horton, 1999). Obviously, if consumers need to spend much effort on learning how to use the complicated navigation, they will not have much energy to absorb the content of websites (Fleming, 1998).

The researcher defined *Effort* in this research as intuitiveness of navigation on websites. Consumers can have optimistic attitudes toward a website if the site can offer intuitive navigation to minimize consumers' effort and is time-saving.

*Pathos*: Three independent variables under pathos.  They are playfulness,
tangibility, and empathy.

1. *Playfulness*:

A study by Webster and Martocchio (1992) found that enjoyment is an important
experience in using the computer system.  Huizingh (2000) also indicated that
entertainment is one of the pleasures sought in using the Web.  Abramson and
Hollingshead (1998) illustrated there are two different Internet users: Surfers or Shoppers.
Surfers visit website as adventurer; they are looking for motivation from site to site.  On
the other hand, shoppers use the Internet for a directed purpose, to gather information for
purchase decisions.  Jarvenpaa and Todd (1996) declared that playfulness means
"shopping on the World Wide Web allows consumers to have fun." (p.66).  Winn and
Beck (2002) explained the function of playfulness as: "A fun and playful website invites
browsers to visit, keeps them entertained, increases their depth of exploration, and
eventually turns them into buyers." (p.20).

The researcher defined *Playfulness* in this research as the entertainment value of
websites.  Consumers can have optimistic attitudes toward a website if the site cannot
only provide information, but also to provide "fun" experience (e.g., games, jokes, and
cartoons).

2. *Tangibility*:

Mary (2001) stated that pictures and words displayed via the Internet will not always
provide the sufficient physical feeling for consumers.  For example, consumers will
usually want to smell perfumes before they make a decision.  Indeed, many consumers
still desire to touch merchandise before buying.  Winn and Beck (2002) referred to this
quality as "tangibility", which is the ability of a website to be able to present wares in
such a way that they have the same appeal that they would in the "real world" – the feel
of that fabric, the taste and smell of the jam.  Winn and Beck (2002) argued the well-
designed websites are designed in ways that compensate for the lack of sensory input that
the consumer has when shopping in a traditional store.  Jarvenpaa and Todd (1996)
defined tangibility as: "Goods and services are displayed as visually appealing." (p.66).
A study by Coyle and Thorson (2001) revealed that a vivid website can provide

sensorially rich content; a site that employs high vividness can more likely to create a similarly direct experience with a product. Watson, Akselsen, and Pitt (1998) noted that a main dimension of websites' attractiveness is vividness, such as: animation, image, and audio.

The researcher defined *Tangibility* in this research as the appeal to the "real world" beyond the boundaries of the site, in a way that compensates for the lack of sensory input. Consumers can have confident feelings with a website, if the site can utilize visual design (e.g., colorful images, 3D virtual tours, and video films) and other multimedia features (e.g., audio effects) to create a "physical" dimension to online shopping, in order to compensate for the missing sensory experience on a website.

3. *Empathy*:

Bishop (1998) noted that the Internet market is " ....into the age of individual markets where each of your consumers is seen as unique person with his or her own needs, lifestyles, preferences, and buying patterns" (p.18). Jarvenpaa and Todd (1996) defined empathy as: "Merchants provide information to reduce the uncertainty experienced by the consumer about the reputation of the merchant and the quality of products and services." (p.66). Smith (2000) declared that personalized navigation can let consumers get their favorite information on the site more quickly; thus, individual consumer could have more optimistic attitudes toward websites, if websites can develop preference information for each customer.

The researcher defined *Empathy* in this research as personalization features on websites. Consumers can have positive attitudes toward a website, if the site can provide individual shopping styles, suggesting products, or services by personalizing the site.

*Ethos*: Four independent variables under ethos. They are recognizability, compatibility, assurance, and reliability.

1. *Recognizability*:

In traditional marketing, consumers' trust is influenced by the seller's buildings, facilities, and personnel (Doney & Cannon, 1997). Geyskens et al. (1996) explained that the traditional firms, who have well-established brand names, can take the advantage of

77

credibility and start their Internet commerce easily. In the online environment, reputation can ensure consumers about a company's ability, integrity, and goodwill (McKnight, Cummings & Chervany, 1998).

In fact, consumers perceive some risks when they shop online, since there is no physical contact as in the real world; however, brand awareness and corporate image can be effective tools to solve consumers' anxiety from the indirect transaction (Jarvenpaa & Todd, 1997). Winn and Beck (2002) mentioned that a strong corporate image, or familiar product brands, can take the advantage of recognizability. Roelling (2001) noted that branding is important because it communicates with consumers by the product promise. In other words, a recognizable brand name can be an effective tool to win consumers' trust easily when shopping online.

The researcher defined *Recognizability* in this research as credible features on websites. Consumers can have positive attitudes toward a website, if the site can show a strong corporate or well-known brand name identity.

## 2. *Compatibility*:

In traditional commerce, the marketplace is a social meeting place that provides benefits over and above the basic purchase transaction (Strauss & Frost, 2001). However, the online format can allow a higher level of dynamic interaction between the companies and consumers, and among the consumers themselves (Sterne, 2001). Online merchants can create social-organizing efforts to bring consumers together. For example, create a BBS network to bring together people who have the same interests.

The researcher defined *Compatibility* in this research as social community building features on websites. Consumers can have positive attitudes toward a website, if the site can help consumers feel that they belong to a community, through the use of offerings, such as chat rooms or bulletin boards.

## 3. *Assurance*:

Cai (2001) stated consumers are aware that their privacy can be threatened by hackers in network of e-commerce. Consumers also worry about the misuse of their personal information when they shopping online (Culman, 1995). Hoffman, Novak and

Peralta (1999) advocated that in an online shopping environment, consumers use credit cards to buy products. If consumers do not trust the online supplier can protect their personal information, they will choose to change to competitors; therefore, trust is particularly important in the online buying experience. Companies need to have an encryption standard that ensures the safety of private information over the Internet. The study by Jarvenpaa and Todd (1996) found that consumers will feel more confidence, if websites display a message that the site employs secure transaction processing. Winn and Beck (2002) stated that assurance is essential to business success, especially if the buyer makes legal or quasi-legal claims on the business. This can include most importantly assurance of privacy and security through explicit claims.

The researcher defined *Assurance* in this research as the promise of privacy and security on the website. Consumers can have positive attitudes toward a website, if the site clearly states their guarantee that companies offer a safe and secure shopping environment.

4. *Reliability*:

Dugan (2000) indicated that the major goal of Internet marketing is to build a better relationship with consumers by open and honest communication with customers. Quality service is a way to begin and foster high-quality one-on-one relationships. Jarvenpaa and Todd (1996) defined reliability as: "Merchants can be counted on to deliver on their promises." (p.66). Winn and Beck (2002) argued ease of two-way communication lines, and a range of customer service options is the rhetorical claim made about good intentions on the part of the business.

The researcher defined *Reliability* in this research as the promise of quality customer service on websites. Consumers can have positive attitudes toward a website, if the site can provide reliable services and multiple open communication channels (e.g., e-mail and 1-800 number). Table 5 illustrates the definitions of independent variables in this research.

Table 5

*The Definitions of Independent Variables in this Research*

| Main Independent Variables | Sub-Variables | Definitions |
|---|---|---|
| **Logos** | Price | *Price presentation.* Consumers can have positive attitudes toward websites, if the site can provide attractive price options to them, such as: price comparisons with competitors, sales, discounts, and special offers. |
| | Variety | *Product structure and display on websites.* Consumers can have positive feelings with a website, if the site can present an accurate representation of products by exhibiting the breadth and depth of product variety. |
| | Product information | *The structure and display of product information on websites.* Consumers can have optimistic feelings with a website if the site can provide very clear, detailed and up-to-date information about products, so as to make consumers' decision-making easier. |
| **Pathos** | Playfulness | *The entertainment value of websites.* Consumers can have optimistic attitudes toward a website, if the site can not only provide information, but also provide "fun" experience (e.g., games, jokes, and cartoons). |
| | Tangibility | *The appeal to the "real world" beyond the boundaries of the site, in a way that compensates for the lack of sensory input.* Consumers can have confident feelings with a website, if the site can utilize visual design (e.g., colorful images, 3D virtual tours, and video films) and other multimedia features (e.g., audio effects) to create a "physical" dimension to online shopping, in order to compensate for the missing sensory experience on a website. |

| | | |
|---|---|---|
| | Empathy | *Personalization features on websites.* Consumers can have positive attitudes toward a website, if the site can provide individual shopping styles, suggesting products, or services by personalizing the site. |
| **Ethos** | Recognizability | *Credible features on websites.* Consumers can have positive attitudes toward a website, if the site can show a strong corporate or well-known brand name identity. |
| | Compatibility | *Social community building features on websites.* Consumers can have positive attitudes toward a website, if the site can help consumers feel that they belong to a community, through the use of offerings, such as: chat rooms or bulletin boards. |
| | Assurance | *The promise of privacy and security on the website.* Consumers can have positive attitudes toward a website, if the site clearly states their guarantee that companies offer a safe and secure shopping environment. |
| | Reliability | *The promise of quality customer service on websites.* Consumers can have positive attitudes toward a website, if the site can provide reliable services and multiple open communication channels (e.g., e-mail and 1-800 number). |
| **Gender** | Males | Gender was divided into two groups. |
| | Females | |
| **Age** | 18-23 years | Age was divided into four groups. |
| | 24-35 years | |
| | 36-50 years | |
| | 51 or older | |

**The important role of Consumer loyalty in Internet Context**

*Overview*

Consumer loyalty is an important concept in electronic commerce. Actually, loyalty has received considerable attention in business literature. Sindell (2000) indicated that customer loyalty is the key factor to decide whether a business can succeed or fail. Newell (2000) emphasized that customer loyalty cannot be brought. Many researchers (Newell, 2000; Sindell, 2000; Smith, 2000) declared that the more often a customer visits a website, the more likely that customer will spend an increasing amount of money on the site. Ultimately, it can establish loyalty and generate more profits for the online retailers.

Most businessmen know it costs more to acquire a new consumer than to serve an existing one. However, many continue to struggle with understanding how to retain consumers. Miles (2000) affirmed that most online shoppers do not have enough time, patience and loyalty, and the situation will not to change much in the future, if marketers can not establish real consumer relationships. In fact, building loyalty should be the core mission, and a long-term process, for marketers (Cutler & Sterne, 2001; Finnie & Radeall, 2002; Newell, 2000; Reichheld, 1996; Sindell, 2000; Smith, 2000). E-commerce is the means of using websites to sell goods on the Internet. How can a company make their consumers loyal in the virtual mall? Actually, in today's crowded virtual marketplace, it is not so much how companies want to communicate with consumers, but how and in what ways, the consumers want to contact companies. Companies need to have the right tools to win the fierce battle (Smith, 2000).

Terry (1999) declared that regardless of whether the firm is a traditional company (brick-and- mortar), a combination company (click-and-mortar), or a pure Web-based company (dot.com), in the online environment, the buyer is king. It is obvious that Web designers must put consumers in mind when they design e-commerce websites. Marketers need to understand the value of shopping online for many consumers is its ability to offer a faster, easier, and less expensive way to do something useful (Bishop, 1998). It means companies need to provide a high-quality website, which has persuasive power design elements to convince consumers to return to their site again and again.

## Previous Researches on Consumer Loyalty

This research examined the design factors on a website that can affect consumer loyalty in the electronic shopping malls. In fact, consumer loyalty has been widely discussed in the research for many years; a considerable amount of literature has been devoted to consumer loyalty issues in the brand or product allegiance (e.g., Brown, 1953; Jacoby & Chestnut, 1978; LaBarbera & Mazursky, 1983; Roellig, 2001; Schultz, 2001). However, the context of these previous research studies did not focus on the Business-to-Consumer (B2C) electronic environment.

In the 1960s to 1970s, many concepts and theories about consumer or brand loyalty were focused on the economics of information, and rooted in the consumer package goods marketing (Schiffman & Kanuk, 1994). For example, Jacoby and Chestnut (1978) raised the topic of brand loyalty versus repeat purchasing behavior in their research. They tried to model how consumers evaluated alternatives and made purchase decisions. Consumer loyalty was usually viewed as behavioral and attitudinal components at that time. In 1980s to 1990s, the researchers' interests shifted to consumer choice and behavior modeling (Schiffman & Kanuk, 1994). For Instance, LaBarbera and Mazursky (1983) observed consumer behaviors in the form of longitudinal purchase occasions. In 1996, Reichheld integrated the loyalty thinking on the economic value over the past several years. He suggested that, "... companies with the highest retention rates also earn the best profits." (p.23). Several other researchers' studies (e.g., Berry, 1995; Oliver 1999, Payne & Rickard, 1997) also had confirmed that consumer loyalty is one of most important characteristics strongly correlated with companies' profitability.

All aforementioned research studies on the concept of consumer loyalty have been developed from marketers' point of views; however, fewer works addressed from consumers' perspective, and ask for why consumers want to be loyal to particular brands. Besides, the marketplace has changed quickly over the past several years. These previous approaches that addressed consumer loyalty in traditional business settings, may be not appropriate in an electronic environment, where shoppers have various choices to products and brands, and are not be restricted by time or geography. The fact is there is not much empirical research that has been conducted to deal with loyalty issues in the

Internet shopping environment to date. It is the time for us to examine and define a new loyalty approach in the Internet commerce for the 21$^{st}$ century marketplace.

This research implemented a rhetorical approach to understanding consumer loyalty in the Internet commerce. The basic assumption underlying the approach is that consumers' intention to make repeated visits and purchases on their current website is determined by the rhetorical function of persuasion on the design elements of a website. In the increasingly competitive world of e-commerce, marketers should understand the important connection between website design and consumer loyalty.

### *Definition of Consumer Loyalty in Internet Commerce*

Consumer loyalty is the dependent variable of this research. Antecedents of consumer loyalty are identified below based on the literature.

Dick and Basu (1994) advocated consumer loyalty being based on behavioral measures (e.g., repeat patronage).

Sindell (2000) defined consumer loyalty as: "the customer's belief that your company is the one to go first for products they already use and for other products they may need in the future…Consumer loyalty includes repeat purchases and more referrals." (p.4).

KPMG International Swiss association (2001) gave the definition of consumer loyalty as: "E-loyalty is the loyalty an online customer shows towards an online business or brand." (p.2).

Swaddling and Miller (2002) simply defined consumer loyalty as: "Customer loyalty is the absence of a better alternative." (p.63). They mentioned that, "customers make a choice each time they purchase. That choice might be between a previously satisfying purchase and the hassle of shopping for alternative." (p.63).

Cutler and Sterne (2001) defined consumer loyalty as: "Loyal consumers come back frequently, buy often, recommend your company to others and really try out new things. They may even come looking for products or services that you do not offer." (p.31).

Smith (2000) defined consumer loyalty as: "e-loyalty…in terms of positive behaviors such as revisits, repurchase, recommendations or active participation in a customer program." (p.22). Smith (2000) explained that loyal consumers not only want to return to your website, they also want to tell others about your website.

Based on aforementioned definitions, *Consumer Loyalty* in this research was defined by the researcher as: A measure of the good faith of consumers to a website. Loyal consumers would frequently visit, make repeated purchases or service, and make "word-of-mouth" referrals to the same website.

### *A Frequently Used Consumer Loyalty Theory in Internet Commerce:*
### *Customer Relationship Management (CRM)*

One of the most important functions that the marketing division of any company can perform is to instill customer loyalty. Customer Relationship Management (CRM) is the frequently used current theory for marketers dealing with the issue of consumer loyalty in Internet commerce. Customer relationship management (CRM) is the customer-centric strategy to establish loyalty with consumers. Effective business strategies have always put consumers at the forefront (Pal & Ray, 2001). Newell (2000) defined CRM as: "a process of modifying customer behavior over time and learning from every interaction, customizing customer treatment, and strengthening the bond between the customer and the company. This is the principle of important one to one marketing." (p.2). For an e-commerce company, one of the most significant tools to establish customer loyalty is the design of the company's website (Sean McManus.com, 2003). However, what specifically about a website design can help to improve both consumer satisfaction and customer retention? Among the ways that an e-commerce company can inculcate consumer loyalty is by allowing the business owner to keep track of both companies' and the consumers' inventories (McQuillin, 2003; Sindell, 2000). Certainly, a well-designed website can help a business-owner assess the customers' shopping patterns, and use this assessment to forecast future buying behavior. Such forecasts can be used to provide better service, and so increase consumer loyalty (CustomerCentric, 2002; McQuillin, 2003).

Furthermore, e-commerce companies can utilize their websites to help the companies understand how consumers perceive their own needs. Wise use of feedback from consumers allows an e-commerce firm to match its own categories with the specific products that meet the customers' needs (Houser, 2001; Smith, 2000).

One company that has been in the forefront of using its website's interactive aspects to adjust its offerings to the needs of its consumers is eBay, since Meg Whitman became the company's CEO in 1998. Whitman's leadership has transformed eBay in many ways: She has used the company's website as a part of an overall transformational leadership style. One of the elements of transformational leadership that she has instilled into the company is the appeal to a high set of moral standards. This is most evident in the company's use of the "natural watchfulness of its virtual community" that Whitman has used to "forge bonds with customers and to police the behavior of its buyers and sellers" (Brown, 2002). eBay has demonstrated the ways in which an e-commerce firm can use a well-designed website to clarify the needs and desires of the customers in a way that is easily operationalized. Operationalization in the context of business is the process of turning statistics and other raw data into information that can be applied to make both short-term and long-term business decisions (Bunnell & Luecke, 2000).

In addition, the website design of eBay encourages both vendors and sellers to be honest with each other and to treat each other well. This emphasis on good behavior is transparent in the design of the eBay website: As soon as one logs onto it one is made aware by the website's design of the importance to the company of integrity in every aspect of each transaction. Many people are uncomfortable about possible security problems in buying online from people that they do not know; such reassurances as to security built in to the website design are important (Bunnell & Luecke, 2000). The rating system of eBay – in which each vendor and every buyer is graded on all transactions – ensures that people are accountable for their behavior over the long run, since ratings remain posted as long as one is participating in eBay. This "individualized consideration" is an essential part of both Whitman's leadership style, and eBay's success as a company, and is a key element of the website design (Brown, 2002).

Certainly, the overall goal of customer relationship management (CRM) is to blend the most appropriate technologies and human resources into the way of understanding the complex and changing behavior of customers (Newell, 2000). Focusing directly on the consumer, and the information that he or she provides, can offer a number of different benefits to a business.  Mitchell (2002) declared that in theory, the purpose of marketing is to understand consumers' needs and to fulfill them; however, in practice, the real meaning of consumer understanding is for companies' risk reduction and investment protection.  The design of the website to emphasize the importance of the consumer's own needs and wants can help a business in a range of different ways, including increasing the quality of customer service, decreasing the time between the initial contact with a customer and the closing of a sale, simplifying both marketing and sales processes, and expanding the pool of customers (CustomerCentric, 2002; Deck, 2001).

Generally speaking, online companies need to treat individual consumers differently in order to earn customer loyalty.  Additionally, customer relationship management (CRM) strategy needs to integrate into all aspects of companies' websites to establish a one-to-one marketing relationship.

### *Five Essential Steps for E-commerce Websites*

Fiore (2000) affirmed that whether companies are doing business online or in the real world, companies need to have products and services to offer first, and then they need to have a place to sell.  In the traditional commerce, the place means a physical store; in the e-commerce, the place means the website.  Bolter (1991) suggested that in this interactive environment, the roles of consumers are more visible and more dramatic than in the traditional media.  A similar echo from KPMG (2000), who declared that online consumers are becoming more demanding, more knowledgeable, and more fickle than before; therefore, real customer relationship management (CRM) should be a key weapon for companies to cope with the tough competition in Internet commerce.

In marketing strategy planning, many companies understand that consumer satisfaction and loyalty are essential to their success, but few companies know how to link their consumer needs and wants with their organizational processes to create the best customer experience possible.  To date, the road to e-commerce success is still a mystery with many problems; one of the major ones is consumer resistance (Smith, 2000).  The research carried out by Parsons, Zeisser and Waitman (1998) highlighted that there are five essential steps for success in digital marketing.

1. Attracting users,

2. Engaging users' interest and participation,

3. Retaining users and ensuring they return,

4. Learning about their preferences, and

5. Relating back to them.

Figure 9

*Five Essential Steps for Success in Digital Marketing (Parsons et al., 1998)*

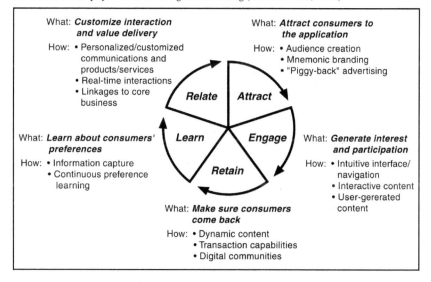

*Attract*

The "build it and they will come" model is not enough to attract consumers in the present day. Companies need to find an efficient way to generate initial awareness in electronic marketing (Parson et al., 1998). Actually, consumers can freewill visit many websites without restriction. Many dot.com sellers use advertising strategy to gain the attention of the potential audiences. Peterson (1999) advocated that when companies want to launch online businesses, the way to driving consumers to sites could be the most expensive promotion. Hwang (2000) illustrated that many online companies spent 25 to 50 percent of their budget on advertising to attract new users. One researcher (Dugan,

2000) found that the cost for gaining a consumer to a website required $30 to $90. Primix Solutions' report revealed that the average cost of an online consumer is $187. If a company uses $40 to attract a new consumer and the gross margin is 20 %, it means the company use $40 to acquire $37 in business (Smith, 2000). That is really not a smart marketing strategy. The high costs of enticing new consumers are wasted if consumers come to visit companies' site just one time, and never come back. Smith (2000) suggested that, "make your first impression count"; it means companies need to prepare a well-designed website, that can deliver a good first impression, and an outstanding shopping experience before they attract consumers to the site.

*Engage*

Once the consumers visit the site, companies need to convert those surfers into purchasers. The aim is to persuade consumers to come back often, and stay longer on the site, because this is the way to drive profits. Culter and Sterne (2001) explained that in the attracting stage, the aim is awareness; however, in the engaging step, the goal is consumer participation. The best way to engage consumers is to make your website interesting, compelling, and entertaining in the way you present your products and services (Parson et al., 1998). Smith (2000) stated that, "…the best e-loyalty program in the world will not overcome the bad website design…A bad first experience on your site can kill the millions you spent on e-loyalty" (p.11). Actually, there is not a second chance to win consumer loyalty; therefore, companies need to ensure each contact creates a positive experience from the customer's viewpoint (Newell, 2000). How to create an effective online shopping site to attract customers to purchase and repeat purchase? Companies need to understand consumers' shopping experience, and create an appropriate environment for offering products and services on the site.

*Retain*

Parson et al. (1998) declared that, "…once you have engaged consumers with suitably interactive and valued content, making sure that they keep returning to your site over times becomes the next critical focus." (p.32). Reichheld (1996) emphasized that high consumer retain can create great competitive advantage to companies. Indeed, no company can afford to keep losing their old consumers. Sindell (2000) stated that consumer retain is the key factor for companies to success in the competitive e-commerce. Although many research studies showed that high profits have a strong correlation with consumer retention, many companies still mistakenly focus on attracting new consumers rather than retaining them (Peterson, 1999).

Companies will lose money from one-time shoppers, if consumers do not come back and make any repeat purchases. Newell (2000) advocated that it costs from five to ten times more to acquire a new consumer, than it does to make another sale to an existing customer. If an e-commerce website can provide consumers with pleasant experiences and keep them satisfied, trust and loyalty can be easily built.

Consumers need to trust a company first, and then place an order. Trust is a necessary ingredient for long-term relationship (Doney & Cannon, 1997). Several researchers (e.g., Newell, 2000; Kimery & McCord, 2002; Peeples, 2002) suggested that trust can create benefits to companies and it can foster consumer loyalty. After earning consumers' trust, customers will refer friends to the website (Cutler & Sterne, 2001; Sindell, 2000; Smith, 2000). Positive "word-of-mouth" referrals are a powerful way to acquire more new consumers, and do not cost any advertising money. On the other hand, if customers feel unhappy with your company, discontent shoppers will tell other consumers immediately. Easely (2002) illustrated that there is an assumption about "word-of-mouth" communication in the old paradigm that every unsatisfied customer will tell seven to ten others; however, through electronic media, the power to transfer bad information is speedy and broadless. It means companies need to pay much attention on every contact with their consumers, and to ensure they can generate positive "word-of-mouth" referrals.

*Learn*

It is not an easy task for companies to attract repeated consumers although marketers know the importance of consumer loyalty. To retain customers and drive new consumers to the site, online sellers need to learn who their purchasers are, and ensure that the company can fulfill shoppers' needs. Houser (2001) advocated that, "Through analyzing information about users, we can gain valuable insights into their problems, preferences,

90

and situation that can later influence our design decisions." (p.177). Parson et al. (1998) affirmed that consumers need a reason to revisit a website. By knowing each consumer's needs, companies can select specific offers that appeal to them. This can generate additional sales and greater consumer loyalty. Bishop (1998) strongly emphasized that understanding online consumers' behavior is critical to building a successful website. In short, gathering important consumer information, and analyzing customers' data to learn purchaser buying preferences is important to online businesses.

*Relate*

Parson et al. (1998) stated that relating is the most important stage in digital marketing. One of the primary aims in relating is to increase the "life time value" of each consumer (Sterne, 2001; Smith, 2000). Value-adding marketing, according to Sindell (2000), is "knowing thy customer" – understanding each individual purchasers, fulfilling their wants, needs, and desires, can increase shopper loyalty; therefore, the customer relationship management (CRM) and customer-centered design play extremely important roles in gaining consumer loyalty.

Newell (2000) explained that, consumers like to be treated individually, and for many of them, personalized or customized sites are the way to go. The more value consumers can gain, the more loyal they will be (Finnie & Radeall, 2002). Companies need to consistently provide consumers real value to establish a long-term relationship, and once marketers have customer trust and satisfaction, they are likely to come back repeatedly.

Smith (2000) advocated that building loyalty is tough because it takes two willing people to build a relationship. In fact, consumers like to have a relationship with a company, only if this firm can win their trust and respect. The loyal consumers are willing to visit over time, promote, and become involve with your site (Culter & Sterne, 2001). On the other hand, if consumers do not feel satisfied with your site, there is a pretty high possibility for them to shop elsewhere the next time.

## *A New Theory Approach for Consumer Loyalty:*
### *Consumer-Centered Design*

The world of business marketing has come a long way since the only maxim was "the consumer is always right". Juran and Gryna (1970) stated that an essential aspect of products or services is "fitness for use". One of the most important new versions of that age-old wisdom is the model of consumer-centered design, and the theoretically related concept of customer relationship management (CRM). These models are used to learn more about the needs and behaviors of the company's customers for the purpose developing stronger relationships with those consumers in e-commerce.

Styler (2000) declared that the motto of consumer-centered design strategy means thriving consumer relationships are the core of all long-term business success. Sindell (2000) stated that consumer-centered approach is the key to create customers loyalty and retention. Designers should investigate the ways that online shoppers interact with computers to build more consumer-centered knowledge. Within the world of e-commerce, an essential part of that thriving relationship with the consumer is an effective website design. In fact, consumer-centered design must begin with customers and grow with online patrons to further develop this marketing relationship (Johnson, 1998; Garrett, 2002; Haig, 2001).

*The Outside-in Approach*

The virtual environment is a consumer-driven marketplace; however, the traditional marketing environment has fundamentally inside-out approach (Schultz & Kitchen, 2001). Relying on sales force reports and formalized market research, companies design a marketing plan which includes only limited information on customer needs or wants. Many believe that the secret to online success is the marketing from outside-in (Haig, 2001; Plant, 2000; Schultz & Kitchen, 2001). This means companies need to pay attention to what the consumers really desire, instead of what companies have created in the past.

Schultz and Kitchen (2000) stated an outside-in approach to marketing communication as: "The marketing organization will have to know and understand how the customer wants to be served, not just how the organization wants to operate." (p.55).

Not like the inside-out approach, this marketing perspective puts the consumer in the center of the system.

In short, an outside-in approach will help companies meet online marketing goals, and build long-term relationship with consumers. Marketing strategies on the Web must be more consumer-driven than traditional media.

*Understanding Consumers' Needs*

One of the problems that businesses have always faced is that managers and owners of businesses have often had only the slightest idea of what it is that consumers want (Drapkin et al., 2001). There are a number of reasons for this lack of knowledge about the consumer. In some cases, it may derive from simply failing to ask consumers what exactly it is that they want, but usually the reasons are more complex than this (Styler, 2000).

Fiore (2000) stated that the difficulty of knowing what a consumer wants are exacerbated by a poorly-designed website but substantially reduced by a dynamic website design. Even when business managers and owners attempt to discern what it is that consumers want, they are often handicapped by one of two facts: often consumers themselves are unclear about what they want; the other major impediment for businesses is that they are not utilizing all the possible sources of information about a consumer (Houser, 2001). Relying only on direct questioning of a customer may or may not prove useful; relying on this in conjunction with less direct methods of obtaining information is a far more robust technique. However, a successful website design makes gathering information about consumers' desires relatively easier than other methods (Fiore, 2000; Smith, 2000).

*Quality Information*

Hirschman and Thompson (1997) stated that consumer-centered design is a powerful tool for businesses, and especially for e-commerce businesses. However, while it can make the difference between a failed and a successful business, consumer-centered design can be highly labor intensive. An effective use of consumer-centered design and consumer relationship marketing (CRM) requires a company to make an overall commitment to a way of looking at its customers as being partners in its own success (Cato, 2001). A well-designed website affords businesses just such an opportunity to work as a partner with its consumers.

Robinson et al. (2000) illustrated that the most important element of consumer-centered design is for the company to determine what information it wants about a particular set of consumers; too little information is certainly a problem, but too much information is also problematic. Enough information, and the right information, is the major key to consumer relationship marketing (CRM), and to marketing success in general.

One of the most important things that a company can do to distinguish itself is to make a long-term connection to a particular consumer. The best way to do this is to have quality information about that consumer. However, while it is necessary to have detailed information, it is also essential to gather this database of personal preferences in a way that does not make the consumer feel that he or she is being "spied" upon. This can be an especially important issue for an e-commerce firm that uses its website to gather information about its consumers (Deck, 2001).

Generally speaking, a well-designed website has the ability to facilitate online companies to gather information in a way that makes consumers want to reveal their personal preferences information rather than feeling that they have to give their personal data (Haig, 2000).

*Using the Information to Improve Future Design*

Having information should never be the goal for a business. Rather, the information that a business has about a consumer is only serviceable if it is being used (Houser, 2001). Information about buying habits and consumer preferences can, and indeed in most cases, should be used to provide better service to customers. One of the ways in which information about the buying habits and preferences of consumers can be put to use is by creating a website that speaks to the need of each customer (Cato, 2001; Haig, 2000; Sterne, 2001).

There are a number of different components of consumer-centered design, and the related larger concept of consumer relationship marketing. Many of these components are state-of-the-art communications technology (Sindell, 2000). Bright (1998) mentioned that many companies design their websites from data-based driven, rather than from consumer-driven. However, while the technical element of consumer relationship marketing cannot be overlooked, it is also a mistake to focus only on the technology (Houser, 2001; Walton, 2002). Indeed, a successful website should always put the end users in mind (Bishop, 1998; Cato, 2001; Haig, 2000; Garett, 2002; Smith, 2000). The strength of consumer-centered design and marketing is that businesses design their websites, and other marketing strategies, based directly on customer information about their own needs (Berry, 1995; Bright, 1998; Johnson, 1998). Perhaps the most productive way in which to think about consumer-centered design and consumer relationship management is that it is an overall process that can be used to help assemble information about customers, as well as information about sales, the effectiveness of every aspect of a marketing campaign, and market trends (Brennan, 1999).

In short, the online merchants must provide a real value to satisfy consumers' online shopping experience. For companies that want to succeed on e-commerce, the most important thing is to design their website from consumers' perspective – to understand their customers' needs and goals first, and utilize this information to design their websites.

### Discussion of the Statistical Method

In order to answer the specific research questions in this research, five different statistical analyses were used. They are descriptive statistics, correlation analysis, independent-samples *t* Test analysis, one-way ANOVA analysis, and multiple regression analysis.

#### *Descriptive Statistics*

Babbie (2001) defined the descriptive statistics as: "statistical computations describing either the characteristics of a sample or the relationship among variables in a sample." (p. 436). Descriptive statistics can present quantitative descriptions in a manageable form. Descriptive statistics are designed to show the characteristic and distribution of variables. It can help the researcher understand the basic features of the data (e.g., measures of central tendency, measures of variation, measures of deviation from normality, and measures for size of the distribution).

1. Measures of central tendency

The central tendency of a distribution is an estimate of the "center" of a distribution of values. There are three major types of estimates of central tendency: Mean, Media, and Mode (George & Mallery, 2001).

*Mean*: The Mean is the average value of a data set.

*Media*: The Media is the middle value of a data set.

*Mode*: The Mode is the most frequently occurring value in a data set.

2. Measures of variation

*Standard deviation*: The standard deviation is commonly used measure of variability around the mean of a distribution. Assuming the data distribution is a normal distribution, the following conclusion can be reached: (1) 68% of values will fall between +, −1 standard deviation, (2) 95.5% will fall between +, −2 standard deviation, and (3) 99.7% will fall between +, −3 standard deviation (George & Mallery, 2001). The standard deviation allows the researcher to check whether the collected data reach the normal distribution. The more the data are spread out, the greater the standard deviation.

*Variance*: The variance is a measure of how spread out a distribution is.

3. Measures of deviation from normality:

*Kurtosis*: Kurtosis is how high and low of the data distribution. A Kurtosis value between +, −2.0 is acceptable in this research.

*Skewness*: Skewness can show how far (skew left or skew right) the data distribute from mean. A Skewness value between +, −2.0 is acceptable in this research.

4. Measures for size of the distribution

*Maximum*: The largest value for a distribution.

*Minimum*: The lowest value for a distribution.

5. Histogram: A Histogram is a bar graph that represents the distribution of a data set. The researcher can examine whether the continuous variables has a normal distribution in this research.

### Correlation Analysis

Larson and Farber (2000) defined that, "A correlation is a relationship between two variables. The data can be represented by the ordered pairs (x, y) where x is the independent variable and y is the dependent variable." (p. 418). A correlation coefficient is a number that describes the degree of relationship between two variables.

The researcher used Pearson product-moment correlations method, which is designated by $r$ in the SPSS software. The value of the correlation coefficient ranges from $-1.0$ to $+1.0$. If the correlation is negative $(0 < r < 1)$, it means two variables have a negative relationship. If the correlation is positive $(0 > r > 1)$, it means two variables have a positive relationship.

### Independent-samples t Test Analysis

George and Mallery (2001) explained that, "A t-test that compares the means of two distributions of some variable in which there is no overlap of membership of the two groups being measured." (p.362). An independent-samples $t$ test can be used when the researcher wants to compare the means on a dependent variable (e.g., consumer loyalty) for two independent groups (e.g., males and females).

### One-Way ANOVA Analysis

Larson and Farber (2000) described that, "one-way analysis of variance is a hypothesis-testing technique that is used to compare means from three or more populations." (p.496). One-way ANOVA analysis is used with one categorical independent variable and one continuous variable. The independent variable can consist of any number of groups. That means one-way ANOVA analysis is able to compare many groups whereas $t$ test compare only two groups.

### Multiple Regression Analysis

Babbie (2001) defined the multiple regression analysis as: "a form of statistical analysis that seeks the equation representing the impact of two or more independent variable on a single dependent variable" (p. 444). Baker (1999) explained that, "Multiple regression analysis is a statistical analysis, which extends the linear regression model,

97

relating one dependent variable to more than one independent variable." (p. 237). Basically, the general purpose of multiple regression analysis is to understand the relationship between several independent variables and a dependent variable.

### Summary

Chapter two provides a general review of the literature of key concepts in this research. A review of literature concerning the use of logos, pathos, and ethos in developing consumer loyalty places this book in the context of previous research. The major gap is that there is a limited amount of empirical literature investigating the persuasive power of website design on consumer loyalty in an electronic environment. The theoretical framework emphasizing a rhetorical approach to assessment of Website design provides the conceptual structure to organize this descriptive and exploratory research.

Chapter three presents the methodology used to answer the research questions.

# CHAPTER III
## RESEARCH METHODOLOGY

### Overview

Chapter three presents a description of the methodology for this research, which focuses upon the persuasive power of rhetorical website design on consumer loyalty in Business-to-Consumer (B2C) Internet Commerce. The research questions which appear in chapter one and three evolve from gaps in the literature. The main purpose of this research is to assess online consumers' feelings, thoughts, and attitudes about the Website design. This research employed the previously unapplied concepts of logos, pathos, and ethos to electronic commerce, as found in the research taxonomy of Winn and Beck's studies (2002), to further examine consumer loyalty.

The research design employed a quantitative method approach, using closed-ended questions on survey instruments. The survey contained 36 closed-ended questions, plus an open-ended question at the end. Respondents rated the questions based on a closed-ended 1 to 9 Likert scale format. By employing a 1 to 9 Likert scale, the researcher intended to make all of the variables continuous. The 1 to 9 scale research design can enhance the likelihood of wider variation of responses than other most frequently used Likert scale formats, such as 1 to 3 or 1 to 5. Additionally, the questionnaire included one open-ended question at the end for obtaining extra comments and suggestions from the respondents. There might be many possible responses for the open-ended question. The plan to analyze the only open-ended question in this research was to group, or categorizes the responses, and ran a frequency count to find if there was any pattern from all of the responses.

The survey was distributed by the researcher to consumers who have previous experience with online product purchases in the U.S. The researcher sent e-mail to potential respondents inviting them to participate in a Web survey. A non-probability sampling (convenience sampling) method was used. This sampling method was the most economically practicable way to the researcher. A sample from Web survey in U.S. was obtained with an "N" count of 307. Data analysis was conducted in a period of four months from September to December of 2005 in the U.S. The data was analyzed using the SPSS statistical program for data analyses, through such techniques as: descriptive statistics, correlation analysis, independent-samples $t$ test, one-way ANOVA analysis, explore, and multiple regression analysis. The level of confidence indicating statistical significance was $p = < .05$ in this research study.

Chapter three begins with defined research questions. A discussion of the research design, the instruments, sampling plan and setting, procedures, data collection methods, evaluation of ethical aspects, and methods of data analyses follow. This research investigated the rhetorical functions on Websites as antecedent constructs that influence consumer loyalty toward Websites. This research aims to improve the lack of quantitative data, by a focusing on discovering how consumers' optimal experiences can be assured by way of the website design. Results from this research provided the insight and perspective to make the important strategy, quality, and operational decisions that are necessary for effective e-commerce implementation. By understanding what people want when they purchase online, marketers can do a better job providing services, and improving the quality of website design.

## Research Questions

The aim of this research was to explore the key factors that explain the persuasive power of rhetorical website design on consumer loyalty in the Business-to-Consumer (B2C) Internet commerce; and how Aristotle's three methods of persuasion (i.e., logos, pathos, and ethos) combine to create a viable, living, reproducible paradigm for $21^{st}$ century consumerism. This research study proposes a theoretical framework based on a modified theory of Winn and Beck's study (2002) that includes three means of persuasion (i.e., logos, pathos, and ethos) to explain how a website's visual design elements may influence consumer loyalty.

The major research questions that were addressed by this study are as follows:
(1) What is the relationship between rhetorical elements (i.e., logos, pathos, and ethos) and customer loyalty in e-commerce websites?
(2) What visual design elements and effectiveness constitute a persuasive model on a website?

(3) Do males and females have different preferences in regard to visual design elements on a rhetorical website?

(4) Will different age groups have diverse preferences for rhetorical elements (i.e., logos, pathos, and ethos) on a website?

In order to answer the four research questions, the research focused on thirteen independent variables and one dependent variable. The independent variables were each linked to one of the three rhetorical modes that Winn and Beck (2002) outline. Four of these independent variables were linked to Winn and Beck's concept of logos or logic. These were price, variety, product information, and effort. Three of the independent variables were linked to Winn and Beck's concept of pathos or emotion. These were playfulness, tangibility, and empathy. Four of the independent variables were linked to Winn and Beck's concept of ethos or credibility: recognizability, compatibility, assurance, reliability. Finally, two independent variables (i.e., age and gender) were regard to participants' information in this research.

The dependent variable was consumer loyalty, which is a measure of the good faith of consumers to a website. Loyal consumers would frequently visit, make repeated purchases or service, and do "word-of-mouth" referrals to the same website.

## Research Design

### *Quantitative Method Approaches*

The four research questions lead to development of a non-experimental survey research study. The research design employed a quantitative method approach using 36 closed-ended questions, plus one open-ended question on survey instruments.

Baker (1999) declared that quantitative research seeks to establish facts, make predictions, and test hypotheses that have already been stated. Babbie (2001) defined the difference between qualitative and quantitative data as, "quantitative data are numerical data; qualitative data are not." (p.39). Anderson and Kanuka (2003) explained that quantitative methods allow researchers using a variety of mathematical techniques to investigate the relationships between the data in descriptions, correlations, significant differences, or multivariate relationships. Analysis is the process that attempts to find answers from collecting data. It may involve one, two, or several variables.

101

Due to the character of quantitative research, certain types of research that study the preferences, practices, attitudes, or interests of some group of people are more likely to be carried out by this method, rather than the methods involved in qualitative research (Borg, Gall, & Borg, 1996). Generally speaking, the aim of quantitative research methodology is to determine whether a particular population shares certain characteristics in common.

### The Strengths and Weakness of Quantitative Research

According to Black (1999), there are several advantages for researchers using quantitative research. The first is quantitative research involves the collection and analysis of data in numerical in form, so the results are more statistically reliable; and the analysis of the results are more objective. The second advantage is that the results are based on large sample sizes that are more likely to be representative of the population. It means the results are able to be inferred to the population. The third advantage is that quantitative methods are appropriate for measuring both attitudes and behavior; moreover, the research can be easily replicated, giving it higher reliability.

The researcher utilized a quantitative research method to conduct this study. The main reason for this researcher using a quantitative research approach is to find out whether online consumers share certain characteristics in the virtual marketplace about website design; and how one thing (a variable) affects another. Many researchers mentioned that quantitative research is all about quantifying relationships between variables (Babbie, 2001; Borg et al., 1996; Baker, 1999). By using quantitative research methods, this research can determine the relationship between independent variables and dependent (or outcome variables) in the sample for this specific research.

The quantitative method design has the advantage of adding more reliable and valid conclusions of general trends in the population, because the results are statistically from a large sample size. However, in this research, the major limitation of the quantitative method design was: the results of this research cannot take account of any unique characteristics of individual cases. This was primarily due to not conducting an experimental research to focus on an in-depth study in Internet consumer patters and habits such as face-to-face interview, observation, and longitudinal or cohort study.

Babbie (2001) clearly stated that quantitative data have the advantages that numbers have over words as measures of quality, but they can have the disadvantages numbers have – poorer in deep meaning than qualitative data.

### *A Rhetorical Approach*

This research presents a framework that is grounded in the classic rhetorical concepts of logos, pathos, and ethos, to investigate how companies might examine the website design for Business-to-Consumer Internet Commerce, and the unique characteristics consumers they serves. The central question to be addressed by this research was how to design a persuasive website, which is able to persuade consumers to purchase products and come back purchase over and over again to an e-commerce site. This research attempted to highlight the importance of a website design based on the consumers' perspective.

Winn and Beck (2002) stated that Jarvenpaa and Todd's article (1996) was one of the first efforts to examine the attitudes of online shoppers. Jarvenpaa and Todd derived three main groups of factors that affect consumers' attitudes toward online shopping.

The salient factors in Jarvenpaa and Todd's research were grouped as follows:

*Product perceptions*: price, variety, and product quality.

*Shopping experience*: effort, compatibility, and playfulness.

*Customer service*: responsiveness, reliability, tangibility, and empathy.

For years, numerous studies have been influenced by Jarvenpaa and Todd's ground-breaking work. In 2002, Winn and Beck, however, further grouped Jarvenpaa and Todd's salient factors within classical rhetoric theory – Aristotle's three means of persuasion to examine how design elements carry out the rhetorical function of persuasion on an e-commerce website. Winn and Beck translated Jarvenpaa and Todd's salient factors to website design, with two different outlooks: "product quality" was changed to "recognizability". Besides, "responsiveness" was changed to "product information". Winn and Beck attempted to make these salient factors narrower and more applicable, in order to measure design elements on an e-commerce website.

The salient factors of Winn and Beck's study (2002) were as follows:

*Logos* (appeal to logic): price, variety, product information, and effort.

103

*Pathos* (appeal to the emotions): playfulness, tangibility, and empathy.

*Ethos* (appeal to credibility): recognizability, compatibility, assurance, and reliability.

The study by Winn and Beck (2002) was the first study that attempted to incorporate all three rhetorical elements, and apply them to commercial website design, by using the qualitative method such as: interview and direct observation. Winn and Beck recruited 15 subjects (7 females and 8 males) who had previous buying experience on the Web. The age range of participants was from 20 to 65. The study showed that subjects had directly reacted to the site's design during their interaction with the interface, and the subjects ensured that there were varying degrees of persuasion by the way that the salient factors were presented on the site. Although Winn and Beck's study showed us these salient factors could have varying degrees of persuasive power to consumers, they did not investigate whether these factors could truly have an influence on the revenue of an e-commerce website. According to a review of literature in chapter two, we know that only with consumers who are willing to purchase products, and make repeat product purchase from e-commerce websites, can companies have profitable online business.

This research intended to extend Winn and Beck's research taxonomy by using a quantitative research method (survey questionnaire) to further measure human experience of consumerism; therefore, the dependent variable – consumer loyalty. The theoretical foundation for this research was established through the literature review of pertinent research. The review included identifying relevant research in the areas of website design, e-commerce strategy, World Wide Web marketing, consumer loyalty, practices of rhetorical theory, consumer relationship management (CRM), and consumer-centered design.

Visual design is the logical persuasive power when influencing online consumers to buy from virtual stores. In order to achieve more specific understanding of the effects of visual design, this research was focused on the relationship between rhetorical design elements and consumer loyalty in e-commerce websites. Using the previously unapplied concepts of logos (appeal to the logic), pathos (appeal to the emotions), and ethos (appeal to the credibility) to electronic commerce, as found in the research taxonomy of Winn

104

and Beck's study, this research can reveal an appropriate melding of the consumer's perception of a positive online experience with a satisfying visual experience.

### *Independent Variables and Dependent Variables*

Given the potential, the empirically-based research on the rhetorical function of website design in Business-to-Consumer (B2C) Internet context is limited. This researcher utilized Winn and Beck's research taxonomy (2002), which is grounded in the classic rhetorical concepts of logos, pathos, and ethos, to investigate how companies might examine the website design for Business-to-Consumer (B2C) Internet commerce and the unique characteristics consumers they serve. The purpose of this research was to show how design elements can carry visual persuasion in e-commerce websites.

In applied research, independent and dependent variables work in conjunction, when developing the persuasive power required to customer loyalty. There were eleven independent variables: logos – the logic of price, variety, product information, and effort; pathos – the emotive response to playfulness, tangibility, and empathy; and ethos – the recognizability, compatibility, assurance, and reliability. When the aforementioned variables are appropriate to the complete human experience of consumerism, the dependent variable – consumer loyalty (i.e., frequently visit, repeat purchase, and "word-of-mouth" referrals) is the inevitable human return on investment (ROI).

### *Definition of Variables*

There were a total of fourteen variables used in this research, which included one dependent variable and thirteen independent variables. The definitions of each variable are as follows:

Major independent variables:

*Age*: In this research, age was divided into four groups: 18-22 years, 23-35 years, 36-50 years, and 51 or older.

*Gender*: In this research, gender was divided into two groups: males and females.

*Logos*: Aristotle described logos as thought manifested in speech. It is the logical reason that the audience finds convincing and persuasive (Covino & Jolliffe, 1995). Based on abovementioned descriptions, the researcher defined logos in this study as: Logos is the persuasion of consumers by using logic on websites. Logos is the power of reasoning shared by the site and the consumers.

*Pathos*: Aristotle used pathos to refer to the form of persuasion based on emotion. This emotional power can effectively affect one's judgments (Covino & Jolliffe, 1995). Based on aforementioned descriptions, the researcher defined pathos in this study as: Pathos is the persuasion of consumers by using emotion on websites. Pathos can stimulate the feelings of consumers and seeks to change in their attitudes and actions toward a site.

*Ethos*: Aristotle used ethos to refer to the speaker's character as it appears to the audience (Roberts, 2000). Based on abovementioned descriptions, the researcher defined ethos in this study as: the credibility that the website established. Ethos can persuade consumers by providing the credibility of the site.

Sub- independent Variables:

Logos: There are four sub-variables under logos (price, variety, production information, and effort):

1. *Price*: Jarvenpaa and Todd (1997) illustrated that price is the total monetary cost for consumers to purchase a good or service, including different transaction costs, such as shipping fees. The researcher defined *Price* in this study as price presentation. Consumers can have positive attitudes toward a website, if the site can provide attractive price option to them, such as: price comparisons with competitors, sales, discounts, and special offers. The goal is to design a price presentation on the website that can support consumers' price-conscious shopping habits, and facilitate consumers making purchase decisions quickly.

2. *Variety*: Podlogar (1998) defined variety as: "... a wide range of goods and services on the site". (p.2). Winn and Beck (2002) advocated that designers should create the ability for consumers to easily find what they are looking for on the site. The researcher defined *Variety* in this study as product structure and display on websites. Consumers can have positive feelings with a website,

106

if the site can present an accurate representation of products by exhibiting the breadth and depth of product variety.

3. *Product information:* Carliner (2002) illustrated that providing information is an optimal strategy for companies. He defined the perfect information design as: "Preparing communication products so that they achieve the performance objectives established for them." (p.43). The researcher defined *Product Information* in this study as the structure and display of product information on websites. Consumers can have optimistic feelings with a website if the site can provide very clear, detailed, and up-to-date information about products, so as to make consumers' decision-making easier.

4. *Effort:* Jarvenpaa and Todd (1996) declared that effort means "saving time and makes shopping easy." (p.66). The researcher defined *Effort* in this study as intuitiveness of navigation on websites. Consumers can have optimistic attitudes toward a website, if the site can offer intuitive navigation to minimize customers' effort and is time-saving.

Pathos: There are three sub-variables under pathos (playfulness, tangibility, and empathy):

1. *Playfulness:* Jarvenpaa and Todd (1996) declared that playfulness means "shopping on the World Wide Web allows consumer to have fun." (p.66). The researcher defined *Playfulness* in this study as the entertainment value of websites. Consumers can have optimistic attitudes toward a website if the site can not only to provide information, but also provide "fun" experience (e.g., games, jokes, and cartoons).

2. *Tangibility:* Winn and Beck (2002) argued the well-designed websites are designed in ways that compensate for the lack of sensory input that the consumer has when shopping in a traditional store. Jarvenpaa and Todd (1996) defined tangibility as: "Goods and services are displayed as visually appealing." (p.66). The researcher defined *Tangibility* in this study as the

appeal to the "real world" beyond the boundaries of the site, in a way that compensates for the lack of sensory input. Consumers can have confident feelings with a website, if the site can utilize visual design (e.g., colorful images, 3D virtual tours, and video films) and other multimedia features (e.g., audio effects) to create a "physical" dimension to online shopping, in order to compensate for the missing sensory experience on a website.

3. *Empathy*: Bishop (1998) noted that the Internet market is, " ....into the age of individual markets where each of your consumers is seen as unique person with his or her own needs, lifestyles, preferences, and buying patterns" (p.18). The researcher defined *Empathy* in this study as personalization features on websites. Consumers can have positive attitudes toward a website, if the site can provide individual shopping styles, suggesting products, or services by personalizing the site.

Ethos: Four independent variables under ethos (recognizability, compatibility, assurance, and reliability):

1. *Recognizability*: Winn and Beck (2002) mentioned that a strong corporate image or familiar product brands, can take the advantage of recognizability. The researcher defined *Recognizability* in this study as credible features on websites. Consumers can have positive attitudes toward a website, if the site can show a strong corporate or well-known brand name identity.

2. *Compatibility*: Sterne (2001) described that the online format can allow a higher level of dynamic interaction between the companies and consumers, and among the consumers themselves. Online merchants can create social-organizing efforts to bring consumers together. The researcher defined *Compatibility* in this study as social community building features on websites. Consumers can have positive attitudes toward a website, if the site can help consumers feel that they belong to a community, through the use of offerings, such as: chat rooms or bulletin boards.

108

3. *Assurance*: Cai (2001) stated that consumers are aware that their privacy can be threatened by hackers in network of e-commerce. The study by Jarvenpaa and Todd (1996) found that consumers will feel more confidence, if websites display a message that the site employes secure transaction processing. The researcher defined *Assurance* in this study as the promise of privacy and security on the website. Consumers can have positive attitudes toward a website, if the site clearly states their guarantee that companies offer a safe and secure shopping environment.

4. *Reliability*: Jarvenpaa and Todd (1996) defined reliability as: "Merchants can be counted on to deliver on their promises." (p.66). Winn and Beck (2002) argued ease of two-way communication lines, and a range of consumer service options is the rhetorical claim made about good intentions on the part of the business. The researcher defined *Reliability* in this study as the promise of quality customer service on websites. Consumers can have positive attitudes toward a website, if the site can provide reliable services and multiple open communication channels (e.g., E-mail and1-800 number).

Dependent variable

*Consumer Loyalty*:

Sindell (2000) defined consumer loyalty as: "the customer's belief that your company is the one to go first for products they already use and for other products they may need in the future…Consumer loyalty includes repeat purchases and more referrals." (p.4). Cutler and Sterne (2001) defined consumer loyalty as: "Loyal consumers come back frequently, buy often, recommend your company to others and really try out new things. They may even come looking for products or services that you do not offer." (p.31). Based on aforementioned definitions, the researcher defines *Consumer Loyalty* in this study as: A measure of the good faith of consumers to a website. Loyal consumers would frequently visit, make repeated purchases or service, and make "word-of-mouth" referrals to the same website.

According to these definitions of each variable above, the research design included an appropriate closed-end 1 to 9 Likert scale of survey questions to evaluate the relationships among the variables. There variables were measured on *The Consumer Loyalty Questionnaire* (See Appendix C), developed by the researcher.

### *Procedure*

All procedures of this research were described in explicit terms so that other researchers will be able to replicate the study. Winn and Beck's study (2000) concluded that a persuasive website design can be described using eleven independent variables. For this study, the researcher defined the research questions to be answered, and then designed an appropriate questionnaire to measure all of the variables. The content validity of the questionnaire is based on a review of relevant literature, and incorporation of ideas from pretests.

The selection of participants depended on their previous online purchasing experiences to answer the questionnaire. That criterion for selection means only the respondents who have previous buying experiences on the Internet participated in this survey. A Web survey instrument was employed to conduct the research. The Web survey was administered via e-mail. This researcher used e-mail to announce the survey information first, and then invited potential respondents to a website to complete the survey. (See Appendix A for a copy of *The E-mail Invitation Letter*). This survey was completely voluntary. Participants may have withdrawn from the online survey at any time without penalty.

The aim of this survey was to help the researcher to explore the key factors that can well explain the persuasive power of rhetorical website design on consumer loyalty in the E- commerce environment. The research employed the following procedures to conduct this investigation:

1.   This research used closed-ended questions with 1 to 9 Likert scale response to design every question in the questionnaire. Survey instructions to participants were as follows: In answering all of the questions, please use a scale from 1 to 9 where 1 means "very strongly disagree", 5 means "neither agree nor disagree", and 9 means "very strongly agree". Write a number in the space provided that

best indicate your feelings about the question.

2. The research included one open-ended question, at the end of questionnaire, to ensure that respondents have full opportunity to express their comments and suggestions for this topic. The research was interested in online consumers' attitudes and perceptions about a website design from a classic rhetorical theory approach.

3. Current research protocols require that all research designs must be approved by the University's Institutional Review Board (IRB) for research concerning human subjects. After the research was approved by Lynn University Institutional Review Broad, the researcher built a website, and posted the questionnaire in a World Wide Web forms on the Internet (See Appendix D for the Web Version Questionnaire). The survey website address was http://mysurvey.hostigntion.com/loyalty/.

4. This research used four different approaches to disperse this survey information, to ensure this research can recruit a minimum of 210 participants.

First, the researcher sent many e-mail invitations to friends encouraging them to participate in the Web survey, and also ask them to help disseminate this survey information to others.

Second, the researcher dispersed this survey information to some popular online shopping chat rooms (e.g., http://onlineshopping.about.com/mpchat.htm, http://chat.yahoo.com, and http://alternativemaketplace.com/chat.htm.) to invite potential participate on this online survey.

Third, the researcher sent e-mail to some schools' professors to notify them of this survey information site. The e-mail contained a hyperlink to the survey website. All of professors could help disseminate this survey information to potential respondents who are likely to have characteristics the researcher needs (e.g., their adult students, friends, other instructors, or colleagues) and inviting them to participate in this online survey.

Fourth, once online with the survey, at no time were participants asked to reveal their identity; thereby, ensuring objectivity on the researcher's part. By using these four approaches to announce this Web survey information, the researcher

111

had no opportunity to know any participants' e-mail addresses or personal information.

5. *The E-mail Invitation Letter* contained a hyperlink to the Web questionnaire (See Appendix A). The potential participants (who have previous buying experiences on the Internet) can go to a specific website to answer the questions, and then "click" the "submit" button to send the response back to specified Internet Protocol (IP) address. All of data were saved at the below Web address over the period of survey: http://mysurvey.hostigntion.com/loyalty/Results.

6. The whole procedure of attending this Web survey remained completely anonymous. The techniques were as follows: First, potential participants received an e-mail invitation to participate in this survey. The e-mail contained a specific hyperlink Web address to the survey website. Using a straight forward process, participants "clicked" the hyperlink to go directly to the survey website. In other words, this Web survey was completed by respondents who agreed to participate in response to an e-mail invitation.

Second, there was no way of knowing which of these participants, who received an e-mail invitation, eventually visited the Web survey page. After participants finish answering the questionnaire and "clicked" the "submit" button, the responses were directly send back from the Web survey site to a specified Internet Protocol (IP) address. The whole procedure was automated to guarantee participants' anonymity. There was no way for the researcher to know who sent back the responses.

Third, the participants were not asked to enter their names or e-mail information into the questionnaire.

Fourth, all of the data was analyzed in aggregate form, and no individual data can be identified in this research study.

Finally, the researcher checked this particular Internet Protocol (IP) address everyday to gather responses from participants over the span of research. Only the researcher knew the password that could access these participants' feedback.

7. By e-mail invitation, the potential respondents were those with access to computer and online networks, who represented the target group - online consumers in this

research.

8. The conduct of the Web survey took four months, from September to December of 2005 in the U.S. There was no compensation offered to study volunteers. This questionnaire collected quantitative data from consumers who have previous experience on online product purchases. This research intended to recruit a minimum of 210 participants, based on the principle that a valid statistical analysis will need to look for about 10 to 15 responses in each of the major sub-categories of the sample for this research.

9. Once the researcher found the response rate was not high enough, the researcher did follow-up requests to different chat rooms every week over the span of the research to enhance the higher response.

10. After getting all responses from participants, the researcher developed a database structure which can integrate the data for this research. The researcher kept all the information that participants provide completely confidential.

11. The techniques for data analysis included descriptive, correlation, independent-samples $t$ test, one-way ANOVA analysis, and multiple regression analyses. For this research, the level of confidence indicating statistical significance was $p = < .05$. The procedures were as follows:

    First, the data was analyzed in a standard SPSS statistical program and ran simple descriptive analyses. Second, the research used correlation analysis to examine the relationship between variables. Third, multiple regression analysis was used to interpret relationships among variables.

12. Finally, the researcher interpreted and discussed the results of all the data analyses, and made conclusions and recommendations for the research.

## Instrumentation

### *Overview*

One instrument was used for the collection of the quantitative data: *The Consumers Loyalty Questionnaire*, which includes a demographic profile (see Appendix C), developed by the researcher. There were a total of 37 questions. *An Information and Informed Consent Statement for Web Participants* (see Appendix B) also explained the purpose of the research and the aim of this survey to potential participants. The researcher conducted this survey using a sample of consumers who have previous experience with online product purchases.

The demographic profile portion of the questionnaire was constructed by the researcher, and was intended to provide background information on each individual in the research. The questionnaire asked for information such as: age, gender, and highest level of education. These types of information enable the researcher to make comparisons and to see whether correlations exist among the variables.

This research study conducted an electronic Web survey. Two pilot studies were conducted to review the questionnaire and its results. The survey with a closed-ended 1 to 9 Likert scale questionnaire was used to rate the persuasive power of rhetorical website design on online consumer loyalty.

### *Rationale of Selecting Instrument*

*Surveys*

Baker (1999) explained that survey research as: "a research method that analyzes the responses of defined sample to a set of questions measuring attitudes and behaviors." (p.505). Babbie (1990) identified that the purpose of survey research is to generalize from a sample to a population. Surveys represent one of the most common types of quantitative, social science research. Generally speaking, a survey design can provide a quantitative or numeric description of the sample (part of the population) through the data collection process of asking questions of people.

The primary advantage of survey research is that it presents all subjects with a standardized stimulus, and so can well eliminate unreliability in the researcher's observations (Anderson & Kanuka, 2003). On the other hand, as opposed to direct observation, the disadvantage of survey research is that researchers must develop questions general enough for all respondents. However, it is not possible to deal with the context, under which the respondents make their choices (Babbie, 1990).

*Web Survey*

The research used a Web survey to collect data. The researcher posted a questionnaire in a World Wide Web form on the Internet (See Appendix D). This research used three different approaches to ensure the research can recruit enough participants its survey. The procedure was that the researcher sent e-mails to different people, and asked them to help disseminate this survey information to others. E-mails were sent out by professors at Lynn University to their students, friends, and colleagues. The researcher also dispersed this survey information to some popular online shopping chat rooms to notify potential participants of this survey information. By sending e-mail invitations to potential respondents, the researcher can encourage people to participate in an online survey. The e-mail contained a hyperlink to the Web questionnaire. When the respondent "clicked" on the link to the questionnaire, their web browser opened and displayed the first page of the survey. A minimum of 210 cases were required for this research. This research planed to use a random selection method to choose the samples if the researcher have chance to gain more than 500 respondents over the period of survey.

Burgess (2001) described that with the growth of the Word Wide Web, and the expanded use of electronic mail for communication, more and more researchers are turning to Web and e-mail options for surveying. The most obvious advantage of Web and e-mail surveys are that they offer the potential for reducing the relationship between sample size and survey costs (Dillman, 2000).

Web surveys and e-mails both involve computer-to-computer communication over the Internet. Most people who are able to "open" e-mails also can access Web surveys. Burgess (2001) illustrated that electronic surveys are placed on computers, and the respondents fill out the survey on a computer, rather on a paper. However, Web survey methods require participants to have basic computer skills for finishing and sending survey messages back to researchers. Obviously, a Web survey is not appropriate for every research, because not every respondent can meet the survey requirement – know how to operate computers.

The Web survey is not suitable for many researchers, since it could introduce bias on a sample selection. The sample may not be representative of the population. For example, many potential respondents who do not have e-mail cannot participate in the survey since researchers can only choose from those with e-mail. The sample is not randomly drawn from the population. However, this sample bias may not be problematic, if researchers wish to survey people who are known to be network users on the Internet. E-mail and Web surveys might have representative coverage in the target population (Anderson & Kanuka, 2003; Dillman, 2000).

The survey is an important tool in the evaluation process. There were several reasons for the researcher to decide to employ a Web survey in this research. First, no mailing costs: It is easy for researchers to disseminate their survey information to potential respondents because electronic mail is rapidly becoming a large part of our communications system. It is more economical to send questionnaires online than to pay for postage.

Second, faster transmission time: It is much faster than the traditional mail method. Potential respondents can receive questionnaires in seconds, rather than in days, as with traditional mail. Additionally, Web surveys offer quicker response time to the researcher than traditional mail response.

Third, higher response rate: Research shows that response rate is much higher with electronic surveys than with paper surveys, because Web survey is easily reached by anyone with Internet access at any time (Dillman, 2000).

Finally, due to the nature of the Internet, potential respondents may be more geographically dispersed, and the potential survey participants are those with access to computer and online networks, who can be representative of the target group - online consumers in this research.

### *Development of the Questionnaire*

According to Dillman (2000), when designing a survey, researchers need to make two key decisions: They first decide whether they would like to employ an oral, written, or electronic method, and next, whether they prefer open or close-ended questions. In this research, the researcher employed an electronic method and chooses close-ended questions.

The purpose of writing a survey is to develop a written set of questions for the potential respondents, and make certain that every survey participant interpreted these questions in the same way (Babbie, 1990). Researchers should carefully consider the type, content, wording, and order of the questions that they include in a questionnaire (Dillman, 2000).

There were several reasons for this researcher to select a questionnaire type of survey design in this research. First, survey questionnaires are relatively inexpensive. Second, standardized questions can help the researcher make measurements more precise by enforcing agree-upon definitions among the participants. Third, many questions can be asked about a given topic. This broad coverage gives great flexibility to the researcher in the statistical analysis.

Many factors need to be considered when writing a questionnaire. This research followed four steps to create a valid survey questionnaire instrument (determine the questions to ask, select the question format, design the wording of questions, and determine the order of questions).

1. Determine the questions to ask:

The aim of this survey was to investigate the aspects of website design that effect consumer loyalty in the Business-to-Consumer (B2C) Internet commerce. This research study was interested in online consumer attitudes and perceptions about a website design using a classic rhetorical theory approach. All of the designed questions must enable this research to successfully obtain the answers of its research inquires. In order to receive specific feedback from participants, questions need to be precise, and not ambiguous. The researcher in this study carefully considered the content, wording, and order of the questions that were included in this questionnaire to make the purpose of the study very clear.

2. Select the question format:

After determining the questions to ask, the researcher needs to decide how to formulate these questions for gathering data in this study. This researcher decided to use closed-ended questions with 1 to 9 Likert scale response to create every question in the questionnaire. However, this research also included one open-ended question at the end of survey, to gather qualitative data. The goal was to obtain a wider range of replies from the respondents. In general, three different techniques were employed in designing the questionnaire. There were closed-ended questions, open-ended questions, and 1 to 9 Likert scale.

## Closed-ended questions

Closed-ended questions limit respondents' answers to the survey. The participants are allowed to choose from the ranking scale response options. By scaling, this research can collect responses with a numerical value for the object. Likert scale questions are the most common ranking scale questions. This kind of question asks the respondents to look at a statement, and then "rank" this statement according to the degree to which they agree or disagree.

The reasons this research employed a closed-ended rating scale format to design the questionnaire were as follows. First, closed-ended questions are more easily analyzed and better suited for computer analysis. Moreover, closed-ended questions require less time for the respondents to answer, so the response rate is usually higher than open-ended questions. However, the major limitation of a close-ended question is that it cannot allow the respondents to explain their deep feeling on an issue because of the simplicity and limit of the answers.

## 1 to 9 Likert scale

This research asked respondents to rate the questions based on a closed-ended scale format. The researcher presented a set of attitude statements to potential respondents by using Likert technique. The Likert technique allowed variables measured on a numerical scale. The research used a 1 to 9 Likert scale to ask respondents to which degree they disagree or agree. Each degree of agreement was given a numerical value from 1 to 9. For example, a scale of 1 to 9, where 1 means "very strongly disagree", 5 means "neither agree nor disagree", and 9 means "very strongly agree". Under this situation, the respondents must decide whether they lean more towards the disagree or agree end of the scale for each question. By employing a 1 to 9 Likert scale, the researcher intended to make all of the variables be continuous. These variables can then be statistically analyzed by the methods of descriptive, correlation, independent-sample t test, one-way ANOVA analysis, and multiple regression analyses. The 1 to 9 scale research design enhanced the likelihood of wider variation of responses.

*Open-ended questions*

Babbie (2001) indicated that respondents can provide his or her personal answer in open-ended questions. The main advantage of using opened-ended questions is that they can enhance research to include more detailed information on an issue. In this research, one open-ended question was included to gather qualitative data. The aim is to obtain extra comments and suggestions from the respondents.

The open-ended question is very useful to obtain free-flowing answers from the respondents. There might be many possible responses to an open-ended question. The plan to analyze the only open-ended question in this research was to group or categorize the responses, and run a frequency count to find if there is any pattern from all of the responses.

3. Design the wording of questions:

General rules applied to decide upon the exact wording of the questions: Keep questions as simple and straightforward as possible. This was a practical consideration due to study subjects' time constraints.

The researcher also considered the following rules to design the wording of questions: (1) Avoid double-barreled questions: avoiding questions that include two or more topics, (2) Avoid questions involving negatives, ambiguity, and confusion, and (3) Avoid asking questions that are beyond the respondents' perceived capabilities

4. Determine the order of questions

Burgess (2001) suggested that longer and illogically-ordered questionnaires may result in lower response rates. When designing the order of questions, this researcher intended to keep the questionnaire logical, short, and easy for participants. The aim was to improve response rate by respondent-friendly questionnaires and easy-to-answer formats. Next, the researcher grouped questions together that have similar component parts to help respondents give a reasoned reply.

Additionally, because sometimes people feel uncomfortable to reveal their personal information to strangers, this researcher placed demographic questions (i.e., age, education, and gender) near the end of the questionnaire, after the respondent has had a chance to become interested in the questionnaire. Finally, the researcher thanked the respondents for their cooperation both at the beginning, and the end of survey, to let participants know the researcher's appreciation.

## *Construction of the Questionnaire*

The survey used for this research was based on previous research conducted by Winn and Beck in 2002. The questionnaire included an *Information and Informed Consent Statement* (see Appendix B) and a *Consumers Loyalty Questionnaire* (See Appendix C), which were developed by this researcher. The Information and Informed Consent Statement included a brief explanation of the purpose of the survey, the confidentiality of participants' information, and clear details on completing the survey. The researcher's personal contact information was offered to ensure participants can ask questions or request further information about this study.

The questionnaire was composed of 37 questions. Questions 1 to 33 pertained directly to the influence of three rhetorical elements (i.e., logos, pathos, and ethos) on website design. There were a total of eleven questions for logos, eight questions for pathos, and eleven questions for ethos. Questions 31 to 33 were designed to measure consumer loyalty of the sample. Questions 34 to 36 were directed to the participants' demographic information, such as: age, gender, and the highest level of education. The last question was an open-ended question. It allowed participants to write down additional comments, and suggestions, and any relevant issues that were not mentioned in the questionnaire. The questions were divided as follows:

Variety questions: 1 and 2.

Price questions: 3, 4, 5, and 6.

Product information questions: 7, 8, and 9.

Effort questions: 10 and 11.

Playfulness questions: 12, 13, 14, and 15.

Tangibility questions: 16, 17, and 18.

Recognizability questions: 19 and 20.

Compatibility questions: 21 and 22.

Empathy question: 23.

Assurance question: 24.

Reliability questions: 25, 26, 27, 28, 29, and 30.

Consumer loyalty questions: 31, 32 and 33.

Demographic questions: 34, 35 and 36.

An open-ended question: 37.

### *Response Rate*

The possibility of bias is less likely if the research study has a high participation rate in a sample selected from a population. This study conducted the following strategies to increase the response rate for this research study:

1. Pretest all questions to avoid problems with wording.

2. Conduct pilot tests to enhance the validity of the questionnaire.

3. Begin with questions that can raise interest.

4. Make questions clear and easy to comprehend by participants.

5. Lay out the questions and answer choices clearly.

6. Employ the convenience sampling method to select the sample.

7. Use e-mail invitation letter to encourage potential participants visit the site.

### Population and Sample

### *Overview*

A sample population is a sub-set of the population. A sample population is used due to researchers being unable to access all members of the population, or because of limitations in time, money or other resources. The purpose of a quantitative study using inferential statistics is to ensure that those who are surveyed are representative of a larger population (Babbie, 2001; Black, 1999; Borg et al., 1996).

Certain sampling techniques are used to enhance the validity of study results. Researchers must ensure that a large number of the selected sample population will reply. In other words, the statistical significance of the relationships between the variables is likely to increase if researchers have a high participation rate in a sample selected from a population.

The researcher considered five major areas of cost such as: money, time, physical environment, human capital, and man hours to decide which sampling method could be effectively conducted by over the span of research. This research employed the convenience sampling method to select the sample. Participants were selected by the non-random sampling method; the researcher selected samples by availability. The main reason to employ this sampling method in the research was the convenience sampling method was the most economically feasible method to the researcher. Since this research study used a sample convenient method, the major limitation of this research is that results of this research may not be generalized to any larger population.

The sampling was conducted over the Internet through a distribution of the questionnaire to potential respondents. This research used a large enough sample size to enhance the likelihood that the sample is representative of the larger population. The research was based on the principle that a valid statistical analysis will need to look for about 10 to 15 responses in each of the major sub-categories of the sample. The researcher conducted this survey using a sample of consumers who have previous experience with online product purchases.

The sample needed to consist of a minimum of 210 participants in the U.S. to ensure the statistical significance of this research. The researcher used the following strategies to ensure this study can get enough sample size:

1. Once the researcher found the response rate was not high enough, the researcher did follow-up requests to different chat rooms every week over the span of study.
2. The researcher made repeated follow-up contacts with friends, and asked them help to disperse the survey information again, to enhance a higher response.

Two different methods were employed to select a sample from the study population. First, if the number of respondents is above 500, a stratified random sample technique will be employed to select samples from the study population. In other words, the researcher will divide these large subjects into different groups (strata), and then randomly select subjects from within each group. For example, the respondents can be grouped into two strata consisting of all male and female. From each stratum, a random sample of male and female will then be equally selected. The second method: if the respondents are from 200 to 500, the researcher will include all of the respondents in this research study.

Eventually, this survey was carried out in a period of four months, from September to December of 2005 in the U.S. The study sample consisted of 307 online participants.

### Inclusion and Exclusion Criteria

The main purpose of this research was to assess the persuasive power of rhetorical website design on consumer loyalty. For that reason, inclusion factors are: subjects who are familiar with Internet navigation, who shop online without unreasonable concern for security, and who are willing to fill out a questionnaire based on their experiences. Therefore, the participants were consumers who have previous experience with online product purchases. To ensure this research study can recruit the suitable participants for the survey, this inclusion criterion was included in *The E-mail Invitation Letter* (See Appendix A), *An Information and Informed Consent Statement* (See Appendix B), and *The Consumer Loyalty Questionnaire* (See Appendix C).

Exclusions included people who do not, or who are not able, to use the Internet for consumer transactions (e.g., vision impaired, technophobe, or non-credit card users), and people unable, or unwilling, to revisit the study criteria over the span of research.

### Data Collection

#### Overview

A questionnaire was used to collect data from consumers who have previous experience with online product purchases. Quantitative data was collected using 36 closed-ended questions with 1 to 9 Likert-type scales, ranging from very strongly disagree to very strongly agree (9 = very strongly agree, 5 = neither agree nor disagree, 1 = very strongly disagree). Before carrying out the main survey, two pilot tests were conducted in order to enhance the reliability of the questionnaire. This research study recruited 307 participants in four months. After obtaining responses from the participants, the researcher developed a database structure that integrated the variables for this study, and then the researcher recorded all of the data into in a standard SPSS statistical program.

*Pilot Test*

The researcher conducted two pilot tests to enhance the reliability of the questionnaire. A pilot test is important, because once surveying has begun; it is difficult or impossible to adjust the designed questions, since the instrument must remain stable in order to standardize the responses in the data set. In this case, two pilot tests were performed with the same sampling procedure and techniques as in the main study. This research study tested the questionnaire on a small sample of subjects first; then asked them if the form and questions seemed straightforward. The aim was to detect any flaws in the questions, remove any ambiguous statement, and correct these prior to the main survey.

The pilot responses helped the researcher test out all the analysis procedures. After doing the pilot test, the researcher made some amendments to the survey that helped to maximize the response rate, and minimize the error rate on answers in the research.

The changing contents of questionnaire were as follows:

1. The rating scale has been changed. The original Likert scale format was 1 to 100. However, many participants reacted that they have difficulty to rate questions from 1 to 100 scale format. The researcher decided to adopt 1 to 9 Likert scale instead of 1 to 100 to make easier rating-decision for participants.

2. Some questions have been clarified for participants to have better understanding.

3. The numbers of questions have been changed from thirty to thirty-seven by separating some aspects to more details.

4. One open-ended question has been added to obtain free-flowing answers from respondents.

## Data Analysis

### Overview

This research used statistical methods to present evidence of the persuasive power of rhetorical website design on consumer loyalty. In the data analysis stage, this research followed four major steps in the conduct of this research:

1. Organizing the data for analysis and validity assessment
2. Verifying the data
3. Describe the data (descriptive statistics)
4. Determining relationships between variables (correlation analysis)
5. Examining relationships among variables (multiple regression analysis)

After the data was collected, the researcher checked the data for accuracy, entered the data into the statistical program, and developed a database structure which can integrate the future measures for this research. The data was analyzed in the SPSS statistical program and simple descriptive analyses were run. There were two purposes of doing descriptive statistics for this research. The first purpose was to clean data and make sure there is no data error. The second purpose was to understand more statistical descriptive information about the collected data (e.g., Mean, Media, Mode, Standard deviation, Minimum, Maximum, Kurtosis, and Skewness).

Next, correlation analysis was used to determine the relationship or estimate the relationship between variables. If the correlation coefficient is close to +1.0, there is a strong positive relationship between two variables. If the coefficient close to -1.0, it can be assumed that there is a strong negative relationship between two variables. Finally, the researcher used multiple regression analysis to interpret relationships among variables. Multiple regression analysis can show the influence of two or more independent variables on a single dependent variable, and can establish the relative predictive importance of the independent variables.

### Methods of Data Analysis

Five different statistical analyses were used in this research. They were descriptive statistics, correlation analysis, independent-samples $t$ Test analysis, one-way ANOVA analysis, and multiple regression analysis.

*Descriptive Statistics*

After data is collected, the first step is run the simple descriptive statistics in a standard SPSS program to interpret the validity on data status in this research. First, the researcher checked the frequency distribution of discrete variables (e.g., gender, level of education). Then, the frequency distributions of continuous variables were checked (e.g., logos, pathos, ethos, consumer loyalty, age, and level of education). The researcher also used histograms to examine the distribution of the continuous data.

*Correlation Analysis*

There are two purposes for doing correlation analysis in this research. First, it can measure the relationship between continuous variables. Second, it can measure if two variables have a high correlation coefficient. If the correlation coefficient is over 0.8 or higher, which means this research does not have two different variables. In order to enhance validity of the research, this study used correlation analysis to ensure that all the independent variables are independent with each other.

*Independent-samples t Test Analysis*

The t-test is used to compare the values of the means from two samples and test whether it is likely that the samples are from populations having different mean values. In this research, independent-samples *t* test analysis was used to examine whether there are different preferences between male and female in the visual design elements on a rhetorical website. Gender is a nominal variable. In this research, it was taken on two values, males and females, which were coded numerically as 0 and 1.

*One-Way ANOVA Analysis*

The analysis of variance (or ANOVA) is a powerful statistical procedure in the social sciences. One-way ANOVA analysis compares group means by analyzing comparisons of variance estimates. In this research, one-way ANOVA analysis was used to examine whether there are any statistically differences between diverse age groups in the visual design elements of a rhetorical website. Age was divided into four groups: 18-22 years, 23-35 years, 36-50 years, and 51 or older, which were coded numerically as 1, 2,

3, and 4. These numerical codes do not give any information about how much of some characteristic the individual possesses. Instead, the numbers merely provide information about the category to which the individual belongs. In one-way ANONA analysis, the researcher is interested in if there are significant differences within any of the comparisons of the four groups in this study sample.

*Multiple Regression Analysis*

Regression analysis represents the relationships between variables in the form of equations, which can be used to calculate the values of a dependent variable on one or more independent variables.

In this research, the regression equation takes the form as below:

$$Y = f(X_1 + X_2 + X_3 + X_4 + X_5 + X_6 + X_7 + X_8 \ldots X_{13}) + e$$

where $Y$ = Consumer Loyalty (Dependent variable)

$X_1$ = Price (Independent Variable 1)

$X_2$ = Variety (Independent Variable 2)

$X_3$ = Product information (Independent Variable 3)

$X_4$ = Effort (Independent Variable 4)

$X_5$ = Playfulness (Independent Variable 5)

$X_6$ = Tangibility (Independent Variable 6)

$X_7$ = Empathy (Independent Variable 7)

$X_8$ = Recognizability (Independent Variable 8)

$X_9$ = Compatiability (Independent Variable 9)

$X_{10}$ = Assurance (Independent Variable 10)

$X_{11}$ = Reliability (Independent Variable 11)

$X_{12}$ = Gender (Independent Variable 12)

$X_{13}$ = Age (Independent Variable 13)

$e$ = error term

The multiple regression analysis shows the results of analysis in the SPSS software as follows:

$R^2$: The $R^2$ indicates the extent of the relationship between the dependent variable and the set of independent variables. Specifically, it indicates the extent of the variance of the dependent variable that is explained by the set of independent variable. The $R^2$ ranges from 0.0 (no relationship) to 1.0, indicating that 100% of the variance of the dependent variable is explained by the set of independent variables. The larger the $R^2$ is the better.

*F statistic*: The F statistic indicates the statistical probability that the relationship between the dependent variable and the set of independent variables could have happened by chance.

*Beta weight*: The Beta weight indicates the unique effect of each independent variable on the dependent variable. A Beta weight is similar to a correlation coefficient. The beta weight can indicate the direction and the strength of the relationship between the dependent and independent variable.

*t statistic*: The *t* statistic indicates the level of statistical probability of the relationship between the dependant variable and each independent variable.

Generally speaking, there are two reasons to use the multiple regression analysis in this research. The first reason is multiple regression analysis can determine the effect of a set of the dependent variables on the independent variables. The second reason is the multiple regression analysis can inform the researcher as to the unique effect of each independent variable on the dependent variable. In other words, it can help the researcher know which independent variable is more important and which independent variable is less important in this research.

## Reliability and Validity

Baker (1999) declared that reliability has to do with the quality of measurement; therefore, reliability is the "repeatability" of your measures. Borg et al. (1996) stated validity means "in testing, the appropriateness, meaningfulness, and usefulness of specific inferences made from test scores." (p.773). In general, validity is concerned about the study's success at measuring what the researchers set out to measure.

Reliability is concerned about the precision of the actual measuring or procedure instrument.

This research employed the following strategies to ensure the reliability and validity of this study. First, this research employed a quantitative research method to enhance the reliability and validity of the study. In quantitative research methods, results that are based on larger sample sizes are more likely representative of the population. This research study used a large enough sample of participants to provide statistically meaningful data, and employ data analyses that rely on appropriate statistical procedures.

Second, this research study employed a structured research instrument to promote the reliability and validity of the study. A questionnaire type of survey measurement was selected in this study. By employing questionnaire, many questions can be asked about a specified topic. This broad coverage gives the great flexibility to the researcher in the statistical analysis.

Third, this research employed a rating scale format in the design of the questionnaire. A survey questionnaire with a closed-ended 1 to 9 Likert scale was used to ask respondents the extent to which they disagree or agree. Each question was given a numerical value from 1 to 9. By presenting all participants with a standardized format, the researcher's bias could be greatly eliminated, and could be more likely to obtain higher reliability.

Another method used to ensure the validity of this research is to conduct a pilot test. The researcher tested the study questionnaire on a small sample of subjects prior to posting online the research survey. A pilot test can help better develop, adapt, or check the feasibility of techniques, or to calculate how large the final sample needs to be.

## Ethics

According to Borg et al. (1996), research means a systematic investigation designed to develop knowledge. Researchers have the ethical responsibility to guard the confidentiality of their respondents. Babbie (2001) further suggested "the fundamental ethical rule of social research is that it brings no harm to research subjects." (P. 38).

In this research, a primary concern of this researcher was the safety of the research participant. A brief introduction was included in front of the questionnaire. The introduction explained the nature and purpose of this research, the procedures to be used, alternatives to participating in this research, and offer participants an extended opportunity to ask questions.

The whole procedure of attending this Web survey remained completely anonymous. There was no way of knowing which of these participants who received an e-mail invitation eventually visit the Web survey page. The participants were not requested to enter their names or e-mail information in the questionnaire. There is no way for the researcher to know who sends back the responses. All of the data was analyzed in aggregate form, and no individual data were identified in this research study.

Data protection and human rights regulation had implications for privacy and confidentially of survey data. The responses were treated with confidence, and at all times, data was presented in such a way that respondent's identity cannot be connected with specific published data. Participants in this research are completely voluntary, and they are free to discontinue participation at any time, without any negative consequence.

### Summary

The central question addressed by this research is how to design a persuasive website, which can persuade consumers to purchase repeatedly in the Business-to-Consumer (B2C) e-commerce websites. A multiple regression analysis was employed to examine the relationships among independent variables and dependent variables. The significance of the overall model was evaluated by examined the R square values. The researcher interpreted all data analysis from the SPSS software, and then made logical conclusions and recommendations for the research. Web developers, consumer-oriented websites, and companies with heavy Internet-reliance for market share results will benefit greatly by this research. The results of this research can make a significant contribution to the development of effective online shopping and supplement discussions in persuasive discourse.

The next chapter presents the research results.

# CHAPTER IV
# RESULTS

## Overview

The purpose of this research was to demonstrate how design elements effect the visual persuasion in e-commerce websites. The basic assumption underlying the approach was that consumers' intention to make repeated visits, and purchases on their current website, is determined by the rhetorical function of persuasion in the design elements of a website. This research examined the rhetoric of websites, arguing that creating an enticing website is possible for any business that attends to a set of fundamental rules of rhetoric. This study focused on factors, which are extremely important from both theoretical and practical perspectives.

The major independent variables were logos, pathos, ethos, gender, and age. Sub-variables for the independent variable *Logos* included price, variety, product information, and effort. Sub-variables for the independent variable *Pathos* included playfulness, tangibility and empathy. Sub-variables for the independent variable *Ethos* included recognizability, compatibility, assurance, and reliability. The dependent variable was customer loyalty.

The research design employed a quantitative method approach, using closed-ended questions on survey instruments. Respondents were instructed to indicate how strongly they agree or disagree with a number of statements relating to their perception of the persuasive power of rhetorical website design on consumer loyalty in the E- commerce environment. A 9-point Likert scale was used (9 = very strongly agree, 5 = neither agree nor disagree, 1 = very strongly disagree).

The survey was distributed by the researcher to consumers who have previous experience with online product purchases in the U.S. Data was conducted during September, October, November, and December of 2005. A total of 307 responses were received by the deadline. In general, the research results encourage the inference of relationships between rhetorical design elements and consumer loyalty in e-commerce websites.

131

This chapter presents the major results assessed from the data collection. Chapter four begins with descriptive characteristics of the respondents. Then chapter four presents results about the relationships among the study variables. Finally, findings are reported in adequate detail to justify the conclusion.

These findings support the purpose of the study to answer the following research questions investigated:

(1) What is the relationship between rhetorical elements (i.e., logos, pathos, and ethos) and consumer loyalty in e-commerce websites?

(2) What visual design elements and effectiveness constitute a persuasive model on a website?

(3) Do males and females have different preferences in regard to visual design elements on a rhetorical website?

(4) Will different age groups have diverse preferences for rhetorical elements (i.e., logos, pathos, and ethos) on a website?

Research methods of data analysis included the descriptive statistic, correlation analysis, independent-samples *t* tests analysis, one-way ANOVA analysis, and multiple regression analysis.

## Descriptive Characteristics of Respondents

A sample Web survey in U.S. was obtained with an "N" count of 307. Of the respondents, gender was divided evenly with 154 (50.2 %) males, and 153 (49.8 %) females. The mean age for those respondents in the research was 32.6 years of age with a standard deviation of 13.59, while 56 % were between 18 to 30 years old. The median age was 29. The age ranged from 18 to 75 years of age. The normal curve for age was skewed to the left with a Skewness of .933 and a Kurtosis of -.105.

Figure 10 shows the age distribution of samples in this research.

Figure 10

*The Age Distribution of Samples in this Research*

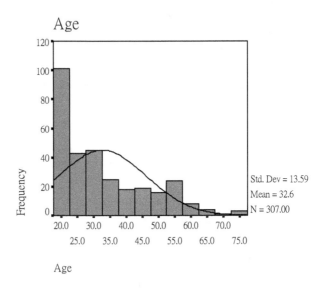

Age

Std. Dev = 13.59
Mean = 32.6
N = 307.00

Age

The divisions of the educational background of respondents were as follows:

A total of 113 respondents (36.8 %) had a high school degree, 94 (30.6 %) had a college degree, 66 (21.5 %) had a master degree, and 34 (11.1 %) had a doctoral degree.

**Research Question 1**

What is the relationship between rhetorical elements (i.e., logos, pathos, and ethos) and consumer loyalty in e-commerce websites?

In order to answer the research question 1, three different statistical analyses were employed. They were descriptive analysis, correlation analysis, and multiple regression analysis.

*Descriptive Analysis for Question 1*

The report of frequencies count about independent variables (i.e., logos, pathos, and ethos) showed that logos had the highest mean score of 7.284 ($SD$ = .5122). Ethos had the second high mean score of 7.192 ($SD$ = .6309). Pathos had the lowest mean score of

133

5.909 (*SD* = .9266). The dependent variable of consumer loyalty had a mean score of 7.447 (*SD* = .5739). Table 6 below displays the basic descriptive data of consumer loyalty, logos, pathos, and ethos.

Table 6

*The Result of Frequencies Count for Consumer Loyalty and Three Rhetorical Elements (Logos, Pathos, and Ethos):*

| Variable | Mean | Std. Error of Mean | Median | Mode | Std. Deviation |
|---|---|---|---|---|---|
| Logos | 7.284 | .0292 | 7.375 | 7.8 | .5122 |
| Pathos | 5.909 | .0529 | 5.833 | 5.5 | .9266 |
| Ethos | 7.192 | .036 | 7.25 | 7.4 | .6309 |
| Consumer Loyalty | 7.447 | .0328 | 7.667 | 8 | .5739 |

N= 307

### Correlation Analysis for Question 1

Correlation analysis was conducted using the Pearson Product Moment technique for three continuous independent variables (logos, pathos, and ethos) and one continuous dependent variable (consumer loyalty). There were two purposes for doing the correlation analysis in research question 1. First, correlation analysis can measure if three independent variables (logos, pathos, and ethos) are independent from each other. Second, correlation analysis can measure if each independent variable (logos, pathos, and ethos) has high correlation coefficient with the dependent variable (consumer loyalty).

As shown in Table 7, there is no correlation coefficient that is higher than .54. Therefore, the three independent variables (logos, pathos, and ethos) were independent from each other. There was no problem with multicollinearity. Multicollinearity occurs when two of the independent variables are correlated to the level of .85 or higher, making them the same variable and completely dependent on each other.

Table 7

*The Result of Correlation Coefficient between the Independent Variables (Logos, Pathos, and Ethos).*

| Variables | Logos | Pathos | Ethos |
|---|---|---|---|
| Logos (Pearson Correlation) | 1 | .341** | .538** |
| Pathos (Pearson Correlation) | .341** | 1 | .466** |
| Ethos (Pearson Correlation) | .538** | .466** | 1 |

N = 307

**. Correlation is significant at the 0.01 level (2-tailed).

*. Correlation is significant at the 0.05 level (2-tailed).

A correlation coefficient is a number that describes the degree of relationship between two variables. The value of the correlation coefficient ranges from −1.0 to +1.0. If the correlation is negative ($0 < r < 1$), it means two variables have a negative relationship. If the correlation is positive ($0 > r > 1$), it means two variables have a positive relationship. As shown in Table 8, the coefficients are positive ($0 > r > 1$) and are statistical significant difference at $p = < .01$ level between rhetorical elements (logos, pathos, and ethos) and consumer loyalty in e-commerce websites.

Table 8

*The Result of Correlation Analysis for Consumer Loyalty and Three Rhetorical Elements (Logos, Pathos, and Ethos):*

| Variables | Logos | Pathos | Ethos |
|---|---|---|---|
| Consumer Loyalty | | | |
| (Pearson Correlation) | .714** | .376** | .626** |

N = 307

**. Correlation is significant at the 0.01 level (2-tailed).

*. Correlation is significant at the 0.05 level (2-tailed).

135

The most statistically significant correlations with consumer loyalty from highest to lowest were:

1. Logos: The score of correlation coefficient between logos and consumer loyalty was $r = .714$ and the relationship was statistically significant at the $p = < .01$ level. This means there is a 99 % probability that these relationship scores were not produced by chance. Among three rhetorical elements, logos had the strongest relationship to consumer loyalty in e-commerce websites.

2. Ethos: The second most significant correlation with consumer loyalty was ethos, which was $r = .626$ at the .01 level of significance. This means ethos was the second persuasive factor to consumer loyalty in e-commerce websites.

3. Pathos: The correlation between pathos and consumer loyalty had a positive ratio of $r = .376$ and was statistically significant at $p = < .01$ level. This means that pathos was the third persuasive factor among three rhetorical elements to consumer loyalty in e-commerce websites.

In general, consumer loyalty had a strong positive correlation to the three rhetorical elements. The correlation between consumer loyalty and rhetorical elements was statistically significant at the $p = < .01$ level, which means they had a strong positive correlation. The number indicates that as the value of one independent variable (i.e., logos, pathos, and ethos) increases, the value of dependent variable (consumer loyalty) also tends to increase. This result illustrates that online sellers enhancing the rhetorical elements of logos, pathos, and ethos in e-commerce websites can facilitate improved long-term relationships with their shoppers.

### Multiple Regression Analysis for Question 1

A regression analysis can determine the effect of a set of independent variables on the dependent variable. Consumer loyalty was the dependent variable in this study. A regression analysis of the set of independent variables result in an $R^2 = .593$. The score for R square was statistical significant at the .01 level. The result indicates that this study has an appropriate set of independent variables to predict the dependent variable.

According to the score of R square, this set of independent variables accounts for 59.3 % of the variation of the dependent variable. The remaining 40.7 % of the variation of the dependent variable are due to other variables not included in this study. Basically, there was a moderately strong relationship between consumer loyalty and three rhetorical elements (i.e., logos, pathos, and ethos). Table 9 below displays the results of regression analysis.

Table 9

*The Result of Regression Analysis for Consumer Loyalty and Rhetorical Element (Logos, Pathos, and Ethos):*

Dependent Variable: Consumer Loyalty

R Square **.593**          Sig.  **.000**\*\*

| Variable | Beta weight | Sig. |
|----------|-------------|------|
| Logos | .525 | .000** |
| Pathos | .047 | .261 |
| Ethos | .321 | .000** |

a.   Predictors: (Constant), Logos, Pathos, Ethos.
b.   Dependent Variable: Consumer Loyalty
      $N = 307$   $*p = < .05$   $**p = < .01$

After reviewing the Beta weight, it indicates that logos had the most important unique effect on consumer loyalty, which was .525 at the .01 level of significance. The analysis shows that logos was a significant predictor for consumer loyalty. The second important factor was ethos, which was .321 with a statistically significant score of .01. It means ethos was also a major predictor of consumer loyalty. The third important factor was pathos, which was .047. However, it was not statistically significant since $p > .05$. The result indicates that although pathos has more or less possibility to be a predictor of consumer loyalty but it is not a statistically significant predictor of consumer loyalty. Taken together, the analysis reveals that three rhetorical elements (logos, pathos, and ethos) have a moderately strong effect on consumer loyalty. That means focusing on rhetorical elements is a positive strategy for dot-com sellers to develop rhetorical websites in order to persuade consumers to buy their companies' products.

### Summary for Research Question 1

Findings in question 1 reveal that three rhetorical elements (logos, pathos, and ethos) had a moderately strong effect on consumer loyalty in e-commerce websites. The results indicates that consumers' intention to make repeated visits, and purchases on their current website, is highly determined by the rhetorical function of persuasion in the design elements of a website. As pointed out by Ehse (1989), rhetorical strategy is a good choice to persuade people by rational, emotional, and credibility.

The correlation between consumer loyalty and rhetorical elements indicates a strong positive relationship to each other. Logos had the strongest relationship with consumer loyalty in this study. As noted by Covino and Jolliffe (1995), logos can be the first thought that comes to our mind when we think about persuasion. Ethos is the second persuasive factor to consumer loyalty. This reflected in Keivn's study (1996), which encouraged organizations to establish sites with the rhetorical concept of ethos, since it can persuade audiences that a particular site is a reliable place to stay and purchase. Pathos is the third persuasive factor to consumer loyalty in e-commerce websites. Howard (1997) indicated that although many people think that the logical thoughts are the main factors to influence our decision making; however, emotions can greatly influence our judgments as well.

Consumer loyalty was the dependent variable in this research. A multiple regression analysis of all variables resulted in an R square equal to .593 at the .01 level. The analysis shows that this research has a right set of independent variables to predict the dependent variable. Overall, the regression results support the inference of rhetorical elements and consumer loyalty relationship.

This finding illustrates that online sellers who enhance the rhetorical elements (i.e., logos, pathos, and ethos) in their websites can facilitate improved long-term relationships with shoppers. Similar findings are reflected in the study of Winn and Beck (2002), which stated that websites need to have the rhetorical ability- to persuade their consumers by logos, pathos, and ethos. Firms that embrace rhetorical elements in their websites create opportunities to persuade consumers to revisit and make repeated purchases, and experience "word-of-mouth" referrals toward their sites.

## Research Question 2

What visual design elements and effectiveness constitute a persuasive model on a website?

In order to answer research question 2, three different statistical analyses were employed. They were descriptive analysis, correlation analysis, and multiple regression analysis.

### *Descriptive Analysis for Question 2*

The report of descriptive analysis about eleven sub-independent variables (i.e., price, variety, product information, effort, playfulness, tangibility, empathy, recognizability, compatibility, assurance, and reliability) shows that among eleven visual design elements, assurance had the highest mean score of 7.564 ($SD$ = 1.1875). Product information had the second high mean score of 7.4 ($SD$ = .7377). Playfulness had the lowest mean score of 3.794 ($SD$ = 1.5266).

Table 10 displays the basic descriptive data of eleven sub-independent variables in this research.

Table 10

*The Result of Descriptive Analysis for Eleven Visual Design Elements:*

|  | Mean | Std. Error of Mean | Median | Mode | Std. Deviation |
|---|---|---|---|---|---|
| Assurance | 7.564 | .0678 | 8.000 | 8.0 | 1.1875 |
| Information | 7.400 | .0421 | 7.667 | 8.0 | .7377 |
| Variety | 7.355 | .0421 | 7.500 | 7.5 | .7383 |
| Recognizability | 7.326 | .0448 | 7.500 | 8.0 | .7847 |
| Effort | 7.296 | .0474 | 7.500 | 8.0 | .8304 |
| Price | 7.084 | .0414 | 7.250 | 7.5 | .7257 |
| Tangibility | 6.997 | .0596 | 7.000 | 8.0 | 1.0439 |
| Empathy | 6.935 | .0668 | 7.000 | 7.0 | 1.1697 |
| Compatibility | 6.984 | .0808 | 7.000 | 8.0 | 1.4164 |
| Reliablility | 6.895 | .0360 | 6.500 | 6.5 | .6315 |
| Playfulness | 3.794 | .0871 | 3.500 | 2.5 | 1.5266 |

N= 307

## *Correlation Analysis for Question 2*

Correlation analysis can determine if there are any relationships between the eleven independent variables. If a correlation coefficient approaches, or is higher than .85, then, in essence, the variables are the same. If the correlation coefficient is .3 or below, there is a weak relationship between the independent variables. A correlation coefficient at or near .0 indicates no relationship between the variables.

As shown in Appendix E (*The Result of Correlation Coefficient between Eleven Sub-Independent Variables*), the correlation coefficients between all of the independent variables were below .43. It means eleven independent variables were independent with each others. There was no problem with multicollinearity.

All independent variables had a significant positive correlation to consumer loyalty, with a significance level of .01, except playfulness. The correlation coefficient of playfulness was .041 and $p > .05$. This indicated a weak relation between playfulness and consumer loyalty, and there was no statistical difference. The correlation scores were as follows: (1) Recognizability: .564**, (2) Effort: .549**, (3) Variety: .529**, (4) Product

140

Information: .508\*\*, (5) Empathy: .475\*\*, (6) Tangibility: .408\*\*, (7) Reliability: .363\*\*, (8) Assurance: .356\*\*, (9) Compatibility: .341\*\*, (10) Price: .332\*\*, (11) Playfulness: .041. Among all the visual design elements, recognizability had the strongest relationship with consumer loyalty.

### *Multiple Regression Analysis for Question 2*

A multiple regression analysis enabled the researcher to determine the degree of influence that the set of independent variables (rhetorical design elements) had on the dependent variable, as well as the unique effect of each independent variable on the dependent variable (consumer loyalty). Table 11 below displays the result of regression analysis for consumer loyalty and eleven visual design elements.

Table 11

*The Result of Regression Analysis for Consumer Loyalty and Visual Design Elements*
Dependent Variable: Consumer Loyalty

R Square **.628**          Sig.   **.000**\*\*

| Sub-Variable | Beta weight | Sig. |
|---|---|---|
| Variety | .228 | .000\*\* |
| Price | .128 | .001\*\* |
| Product Information | .125 | .005\*\* |
| Effort | .165 | .000\*\* |
| Playfulness | -.082 | .029\* |
| Tangibility | .102 | .025\* |
| Empathy | .100 | .029\* |
| Recognizability | .195 | .000\*\* |

| | | |
|---|---|---|
| Compatibility | .096 | .025* |
| Assurance | .111 | .004** |
| Reliability | .117 | .003** |

a.  Predictors: (Constant), Reliability, Empathy, Assurance, Tangibility, Price, Variety,
    Playfulness, Recognizability, Product Information, Compatibility, Effort
b.  Dependent Variable: Consumer Loyalty
    $N = 307$  $*p = < .05$  $**p = < .01$

The R square ranges from 0.0 (no relationship) to 1.0, indicating that 100% of the variance of the dependent variable is explained by the set of independent variables. As can be seen in Table 12, the R square is .628 with an overall significant at the .01 level, which made the findings statistically robust. Overall, this set of independent variables accounts for 62.8 % of the variation of the dependent variable (consumer loyalty). The remaining 37.2 % of the variation of the dependent variable are due to other variables not included in this research.

After reviewing the regression analysis, Beta weight presents the level at which the independent variable is a predictor of the dependent variable. The score of Beta weight showed that among eleven independent variables, ten visual design elements had positive statistical significant persuasive ability to consumers to be loyal toward an e-commerce website. Only one visual design element (playfulness) had a negative influence on consumer loyalty. As to consumer loyalty, the strongest predictors from highest to lowest were:

1. Variety: Variety had a positive standardized Beta weight with consumer loyalty. The score was .228 at the .01 level of significance ( $p = .000$). In the questionnaire, two questions (question 1 and 2) were related to variety. The question 2 ($M = 7.56$) had a higher mean score than question 1 ($M = 7.15$). Participants felt that they would likely make repeated purchases from a website if the site can help them to quickly find the product that they want.

2. Recognizability: Recognizability had a positive standardized Beta weight with consumer loyalty. The score was .195 at the .01 level of significance ( $p = .000$). Two questions (question 19 and 20) were designed to measure

142

recognizability in the questionnaire. The question 19 ($M = 7.34$) had a little higher mean score than question 20 ($M = 7.32$). Participants reacted that they would likely make repeated purchases from a website if the site has strong corporate image that they can recognize.

3. Effort: Effort had a positive standardized Beta weight with consumer loyalty. The score was .195 at the .01 level of significance ($p = .000$). In the questionnaire, there were two questions (question 10 and 11) related to effort. The question 11 ($M = 7.65$) had a higher mean score than question 10 ($M = 6.94$). Respondents felt they would likely make repeated purchases from a website if they can complete their online shopping with little or no difficulty. Subject 38 had a following comment illustrated this design solution positively: "In general, I feel that the "feel" of a website is more important than the "look" of a website. In other words, navigation logicalness is preferred over fancy graphics or multi-media content."

4. Price: Price had a positive standardized Beta weight with consumer loyalty. The score was .128 at the .01 level of significance ($p = .001$). Four questions (question 3, 4, 5, and 6) were related to price in the questionnaire. The question 3 ($M = 7.42$) and 4 ($M = 7.21$) had the highest mean scores than other questions. Participants reacted that they would likely make repeated purchases from a website if the site shows them its discount price, shipping price, and comparisons with competitors' price. Subject 262 had a following comment illustrated this design solution as: "My biggest frustration is that I do not know approximate shipping charges until very late in the ordering process." The strategy of revealing all costs in the first order page (e.g., shipping fee) on a website is also a powerful tool for Web designer to convince online consumers.

5. Product information: Product information had a positive standardized Beta weight with consumer loyalty. The score was .125 at the .01 level of significance ($p = .005$). In the questionnaire, three questions (question 7, 8 and 9) were related to product information. The question 9 ($M = 7.56$) had a highest mean score than question 7 and 8. Participants felt that they would likely

make repeated purchases from a website if the site can make all product information easy to find and read.

6. Reliability: Reliability had a positive standardized Beta weight, which was .117 with a statistically significant score of .003 ($p = < .01$). In the questionnaire, there were six questions (question 25, 26, 27, 28, 29, and 30) related to reliability. The question 25 ($M = 7.94$) had the highest mean score than other questions. Participants felt that they would likely make repeated purchases from the website if they were ensured that the company offers good customer service. Subject 64 had a positive comment for this issue as: "Assurance from company is to guarantee complete satisfaction or money back guarantee, complete with shipping and handling coverage for returned items." Subject 78 wrote a comment as: "When using the Internet, safety, and speed of delivery are my priority consideration."

7. Assurance: Assurance had a positive standardized Beta weight, which was .111 with a statistically significant score of .004 ($p = < .01$). One question (question 24) was related to assurance in the questionnaire, which had a mean score of 7.64. Participants felt that they would likely make repeated purchases from a website if the site includes clear statements assuring privacy and security. Subject 42 had a following comment illustrated this design solution: "I hate junk mails! I need my privacy; please do not sell my e-mail address or personal information to any company."

8. Tangibility: Tangibility had a positive standardized Beta weight, which was .102 ($p = .025$). It was statistically significant since $p = < .05$. Three questions (question 16, 17, and 18) were designed to measure tangibility in the questionnaire. The question 16 ($M = 7.60$) had a higher mean score than other questions. Participants reacted that they would likely make repeated purchases from a website if the site has many colorful pictures to help them make purchase decision. Subject 67 had the comment about this issue as: "I like a colorful and aesthetically pleasing Web design. However, it is better to lack of pop-up ads (very annoying)."

9. Empathy: Empathy had a positive standardized Beta weight, which was .100 with a statistically significant score of .029 ( $p = < .05$ ). In the questionnaire, one question (question 23) related to product empathy, which had a mean score of 6.93. Respondents felt that they would likely make repeated purchases from a website if the site can learn their individual buying pattern and offers them more useful purchasing information based on that learning. Subject 283 had a comment about this issue: "Don't make me think too much! Learn my personal shopping style."

10. Compatibility: Compatibility had a positive Beta weight with consumer loyalty. The score was .096 at the .05 level of significance ( $p = .025$ ). Two questions (question 21 and 22) were designed to measure tangibility in the questionnaire. The question 21 ($M = 7.37$) had a higher mean score than question 22 ($M = 6.60$). Participants reacted that they would likely make repeated purchases from a website if the site offers them connections to other buyers of this product (i.e., through bulletin boards or chat rooms). Subject 111 had following comment as: "I think websites that are selling high end merchandise such as automobiles should offer a live chat or video conference option to potential buyers."

11. Playfulness: Playfulness had a negative Beta weight. The score was -.082 at the .05 level of significance ( $p = .029$ ). In the questionnaire, four questions (question 12, 13, 14, and 15) were related to playfulness. The question 15 ($M = 4.49$) had the highest mean score than other questions. Respondents felt that they would likely make repeated purchases from a website if the site changes entertaining elements frequently.

According to aforementioned findings, variety was the most important factor in logos. Recognizability was the most significant factor in ethos. Tangibility was the most salient factor in pathos.

### Summary for Research Question 2

Findings in question 2 reveal that eleven visual design elements (i.e., price, variety, product information, effort, playfulness, tangibility, empathy, recognizability, compatibility, assurance, and reliability) had a moderately strong effect on consumer loyalty in e-commerce websites. The R square was .628 with an overall significant at the .01 level, which made the findings statistically robust. That means these visual design elements and their effectiveness can really constitute a persuasive model on a website.

The Beta weight addressed the answer to the second question for this research.

What visual design elements and effectiveness constitute a persuasive model on a website?

The strongest predictor of consumer loyalty was variety, which had a positive standardized Beta weight with consumer loyalty. The score was .228 at the .01 level of significance. Variety means product structure and display on websites in this research. Consumers can have positive feelings with a website, if the site can present an accurate representation of products by exhibiting the breadth and depth of product variety. This result reflected in Podlogar's (1998) research, which stated that a successful website needs to have a wide range of goods and service.

The weakest predictor of consumer loyalty was playfulness, which had a negative Beta weight. The score was -.082 at the .05 level of significance. The number indicates that as the value of playfulness increases, the value of consumer loyalty tends to decrease. This finding is unexpected by the researcher. That means a playful website does not appear to have been a positive dominant factor in building consumer loyalty on e-commerce websites. Being able to play games, read jokes, or watch cartoons on the website might allow consumers to have fun. However, the problem with the playful approach is that many shoppers are goal-focus consumers. They do not have endless amounts of time. Wolfinbarger and Gilly (2001) explained that, "goal-oriented or utilitarian shoppers are transaction-oriented and desire to purchase what they want quickly and without distraction" (p.34). Subject 104 wrote a comment for this issue as: "I think the primary value of a Web design is clarity. It is better to avoid distracting "bells and whistles"." This could be the reason why the independent variable – playfulness has a negative relationship with consumer loyalty on an e-commerce website in this research.

## Research Question 3

Do males and females have different preferences in regard to visual design elements on a rhetorical website?

In order to answer the research question 3, independent-samples *t* test analysis was utilized. The independent-samples *t* test can compare the means of two different groups (i.e., males and females). This analysis also can determine if the means of two groups' distributions differ significantly from each other.

### *Independent-samples t Test Analysis for Question 3*

The final data-producing sample consists of 307 participants who completed the survey; including 154 (50.2 %) males and 153 (49.8 %) females. Gender is a nominal variable. In this research, it was taken on two values, males and females, which were coded numerically as 0 and 1.

Table 12 below displays the mean scores for males and females on different visual design elements in this research. The table also displays the results of the two-tailed significant difference between males and females.

Table 12

*The Result of Independent-samples t Test for Males and Females*

| Variable | Males (N = 154) Mean | Females (N = 153) Mean | Sig. (two-tailed) |
|---|---|---|---|
| Variety | 7.354 | 7.356 | .601 |
| Price | 7.106 | 7.062 | .43 |
| Information | 7.348 | 7.451 | .224 |
| Effort | 7.269 | 7.324 | .569 |
| Playfulness | 4.031 | 3.556 | .006** |
| Tangibility | 6.950 | 7.044 | .434 |
| Empathy | 6.974 | 6.895 | .557 |
| Recognizability | 7.231 | 7.422 | .033* |

| | | | |
|---|---|---|---|
| Compatibility | 7.039 | 6.928 | .494 |
| Assurance | 7.519 | 7.608 | .515 |
| Reliability | 6.906 | 6.885 | .768 |

$*p = < .05$    $**p = < .01$

The final result shows that among eleven visual design elements, only two design elements (playfulness and recognizability) had significant difference between males and females. In playfulness, the independent-samples $t$ test analysis indicates that the 154 males had a mean of 4.031; the 153 females had a mean of 3.556 in this research, which had the score of mean difference .475. The means differ significantly at the $p < .01$ level ( $p = .006$). In recognizability, the independent-samples $t$ test analysis indicates that the 154 males had a mean of 7.231; the 153 females had a mean of 7.422 in this research, which had the score of mean difference -.191. The means differ significantly at the $p < .05$ level ( $p = .033$).

### Summary for Research Question 3

According to abovementioned findings, among eleven visual design elements, there were no significant differences between males and females in nine design elements. The nine design elements were price, variety, product information, effort, tangibility, empathy, compatibility, assurance, and reliability.

However, males and females differed significantly from each other in the visual elements of playfulness on a rhetorical website. Jarvenpaa and Todd (1996) declared that playfulness means "shopping on the World Wide Web allows consumers to have fun." (p.66). This finding indicated that males prefer the "fun" experiences than females in using the Web. Haig (2000) gave a suggestion to online dealers before designing their website. He mentioned the importance of defining the websites' target audiences first, then developing the content and character of websites. Generally speaking, online shoppers are very diverse. The results of this research have highlighted the importance of embracing a consumer-centered design approach when developing e-commerce strategies. This research indicates that if an online dealer's target audiences are males, he or she could consider creating a website not only to provide information, but also to have more entertainment factors, in order to attract male audiences' visit.

Males and females also were significant different from each other in the visual elements of recognizability on a rhetorical website. This means that females were more concerned with strong corporate images and famous brand names than males in using the Web. Mcknight, Cummings and Chervany (1998) explained that a strong corporate image can ensure consumers about a company's integrity in the online environment. This result can help us understand that online sellers, who have high-quality reputations, can take the advantage of credibility and start their Internet commerce more easily with female audiences.

**Research Question 4**

Will different age groups have diverse preferences for rhetorical elements (i.e., logos, pathos, and ethos) on a website?

In order to answer the research question 4, one statistical analysis was employed. It was One-way ANOVA analysis.

*One-way ANOVA Analysis for Question 4*

In this research study, age was divided into four groups: 18-22 years, 23-35 years, 36-50 years, and 51 or older, which were coded numerically as 1, 2, 3, and 4. One-way ANOVA analysis was used to examine whether there are any statistical differences between diverse age groups in the rhetorical elements of a website. Post Hoc tests include a Scheffe test to identify between which groups differ significantly from each other. The detail analyses of each variable are below.

*One-way ANOVA Analysis for Logos*

Based on the ANOVA table 13, there were no significant difference existed among the four groups ( $p = .091$ ). The mean difference between each groups also were not statistically significance. (See Appendix F- *ANOVA Analysis: Descriptive Information of Each Age Group*). Since $p > .05$, there were no significant differences in the rhetorical element of logos among four age groups in this research.

149

Table 13

*ANOVA and Post Hoc Comparisons of Significant Differences for Logos.*

**ANOVA**

LOGOS

|  | Sum of Squares | df | Mean Square | F | Sig. |
|---|---|---|---|---|---|
| Between Groups | 1.691 | 3 | .564 | 2.173 | .091 |
| Within Groups | 78.587 | 303 | .259 | | |
| Total | 80.278 | 306 | | | |

**Multiple Comparisons**

Dependent Variable: LOGOS
Scheffe

| (I) AGEGROUP | (J) AGEGROUP | Mean Difference (I-J) | Std. Error | Sig. |
|---|---|---|---|---|
| 1 | 2 | .027 | .0710 | .986 |
|  | 3 | -.123 | .0848 | .554 |
|  | 4 | .132 | .0913 | .555 |
| 2 | 1 | -.027 | .0710 | .986 |
|  | 3 | -.149 | .0843 | .371 |
|  | 4 | .105 | .0907 | .719 |
| 3 | 1 | .123 | .0848 | .554 |
|  | 2 | .149 | .0843 | .371 |
|  | 4 | .255 | .1020 | .103 |
| 4 | 1 | -.132 | .0913 | .555 |
|  | 2 | -.105 | .0907 | .719 |
|  | 3 | -.255 | .1020 | .103 |

1= 18-22 years   2= 23-35 years   3= 36-50 years   4= 51 or older

*One-way ANOVA Analysis for Pathos*

Table 14 below displays the result of ANOVA analysis. There were significant difference existed among the four groups at the .01 level. In Table 14, the asterisks (*) indicate four groups have means differ significantly ( $p = < .05$ ) from each other (See Appendix F- *ANOVA Analysis: Descriptive Information of Each Age Group*).

According to the descriptive data, age group 1 had the highest mean score ($M = 6.433$) than other groups in pathos. Age group 4 had the lowest mean score ($M = 4.711$) than other groups in pathos. The result indicates that among four age groups, age group 1 (18-22 years) were more like emotional factors (i.e., playfulness, tangibility, and empathy) than other groups on a website. On the other hand, age group 4 (51 or older) paid less attention to the emotional factors in using the Web.

Table 14

*ANOVA and Post Hoc Comparisons of Significant Differences for Pathos.*

**ANOVA**

PATHOS

|  | Sum of Squares | df | Mean Square | F | Sig. |
|---|---|---|---|---|---|
| Between Groups | 99.921 | 3 | 33.307 | 61.983 | .000 |
| Within Groups | 162.821 | 303 | .537 | | |
| Total | 262.742 | 306 | | | |

**Multiple Comparisons**

Dependent Variable: PATHOS
Scheffe

| (I) AGEGROUP | (J) AGEGROUP | Mean Difference (I-J) | Std. Error | Sig. |
|---|---|---|---|---|
| 1 | 2 | .361* | .1022 | .007 |
|   | 3 | .816* | .1221 | .000 |
|   | 4 | 1.722* | .1314 | .000 |
| 2 | 1 | -.361* | .1022 | .007 |
|   | 3 | .455* | .1213 | .003 |
|   | 4 | 1.361* | .1306 | .000 |
| 3 | 1 | -.816* | .1221 | .000 |
|   | 2 | -.455* | .1213 | .003 |
|   | 4 | .906* | .1468 | .000 |
| 4 | 1 | -1.722* | .1314 | .000 |
|   | 2 | -1.361* | .1306 | .000 |
|   | 3 | -.906* | .1468 | .000 |

*. The mean difference is significant at the .05 level.

1= 18-22 years    2= 23-35 years    3= 36-50 years    4= 51 or older

*One-way ANOVA Analysis for Ethos*

Based on the ANOVA table 15, $p = .000$, there was significant difference existed among the four groups. In Table 15, the asterisks (*) indicate there were three pairs of groups (group 1 and group 4, group 2 and group 4, group 3 and group 4) whose means differ significantly ( $p = < .05$) from each other. According to the descriptive data (See Appendix F- *ANOVA Analysis: Descriptive Information of Each Age Group*), group 1 had the highest mean score ($M = 7.375$) than other groups in ethos. Group 1 also had mean differ significantly with group 4 ($M = 6.606$). There were no mean differ significantly between group 1 and group 2($M = 7.232$). There were no mean differ significantly between group 1 and group 3($M = 7.258$). The result indicates that among four age groups, age group1 (18-22 years) paid much attention to the trustworthy (i.e., recognizability, compatibility, assurance, and reliability) that the website established. Group 4 (51 or older) paid less attention to the credibility factors in using the Web.

Table 15

*ANOVA and Post Hoc Comparisons of Significant Differences for Ethos.*

**ANOVA**

ETHOS

|  | Sum of Squares | df | Mean Square | F | Sig. |
|---|---|---|---|---|---|
| Between Groups | 19.285 | 3 | 6.428 | 19.001 | .000 |
| Within Groups | 102.512 | 303 | .338 |  |  |
| Total | 121.797 | 306 |  |  |  |

**Multiple Comparisons**

Dependent Variable: ETHOS
Scheffe

| (I) AGEGROUP | (J) AGEGROUP | Mean Difference (I-J) | Std. Error | Sig. |
|---|---|---|---|---|
| 1 | 2 | .144 | .0811 | .372 |
|  | 3 | .117 | .0969 | .691 |
|  | 4 | .770* | .1042 | .000 |
| 2 | 1 | -.144 | .0811 | .372 |
|  | 3 | -.026 | .0962 | .995 |
|  | 4 | .626* | .1036 | .000 |
| 3 | 1 | -.117 | .0969 | .691 |
|  | 2 | .026 | .0962 | .995 |
|  | 4 | .653* | .1164 | .000 |
| 4 | 1 | -.770* | .1042 | .000 |
|  | 2 | -.626* | .1036 | .000 |
|  | 3 | -.653* | .1164 | .000 |

*. The mean difference is significant at the .05 level.

1= 18-22 years    2= 23-35 years    3= 36-50 years    4= 51 or older

153

## Summary for Research Question 4

The final results show that there were no diverse preferences for the rhetorical element of logos among four age groups in this research. However, significant differences existed among the four groups for rhetorical elements of pathos and ethos. Age group1 (18-22 years) preferred emotional factors (i.e., playfulness, tangibility, and empathy) and trustworthy factors (i.e., recognizability, compatibility, assurance, and reliability) than other groups in using a website. On the other hand, group 4 (51 or older) paid less attention to the emotional factors and trustworthy factors in using the Web.

## Analysis of the Open-ended Question

In the questionnaire, the researcher added an open-ended question to ask online participants if they have any additional suggestions regarding website design. The original plan to analyze the open-ended question was to group or categorize the responses, and run a frequency count. The aim was to find any difference in thinking from all of the responses. However, there were only 21 participants who wrote comments for the open-ended question. All of their suggestions and ideas were related to the rhetorical approach in this research study. Only two comments were not included by this research. They were related to the advertising topic. Although online adverting design is a very important issue to the internet commerce, it is not the main subject in this paper. Since there were not many free-flowing comments from participants, the need to run a frequency count for analyzing the open-ended question was diminished. The researcher gathered all the participants' suggestions in appendix G. Please see appendix G: *The Open-ended Question: Comments by Subjects.*

The next chapter presents conclusions of the research.

# CHAPTER V
## SUMMARY, FINDINGS, DISCUSSION, IMPLICATIONS, FURTHE
## RESEARCH, AND CONCLUSIONS

Chapter five briefly provides a final review of the research. The subsequent sections summarized the motivation of the research, the statistical findings, a discussion of results, limitations of the research, practical implications of the findings, conclusions, and suggestions for future research were discussed.

**Summary of the Research**

Electronic commerce is rising speedily. Unrestricted by time, distance, and physical location, the online shopping malls have captured many attentions of marketers. However, while the Internet may offer marketers a new way of doing business, it is far from mature, and the global competition has increased dramatically. Many companies entered e-commerce in quite a rush, without valuable strategies on hand. Then, we witnessed the rise and fall of many dot.com companies. Obviously more sophisticated perspectives must be brought to this subject.

A website allows companies doing business on a worldwide level. Marketers use website designs to communicate with their potential customers. The aim is to persuade consumers to visit, come back frequently, stay longer, and finally purchase on the site, because this is the way to drive profits. Although many marketers know the importance of customer loyalty, it is not an easy task for companies to achieve. Consumer loyalty is the relationship between a consumer and a company, and this relationship needs to be nurtured and managed. Therefore, this research presents a framework that is grounded in the classical rhetorical concepts of logos, pathos, and ethos to examine consumer loyalty. The expectation was that enhancing the design elements of logos, pathos, and ethos would increase consumers' optimistic feeling, and lead to loyal attitudes toward the website. Websites that operate on the basis of rational, emotional, and credible ways have better chances to win consumers' hearts.

This research addressed the following questions:

(1) What is the relationship between rhetorical elements (i.e., logos, pathos, and ethos) and customer loyalty in e-commerce websites?

(2) What visual design elements and effectiveness constitute a persuasive model on a website?

(3) Do males and females have different preferences in regard to visual design elements on a rhetorical website?

(4) Will different age groups have different preferences for rhetorical elements (i.e., logos, pathos, and ethos) on a website?

In order to answer the four research questions, the research focused on thirteen independent variables and one dependent variable. The major independent variables were logos, pathos, ethos, gender, and age. Sub-variables for the independent variable *Logos* included price, variety, product information, and effort. Sub-variables for the independent variable *Pathos* included playfulness, tangibility and empathy. Sub-variables for the independent variable *Ethos* included recognizability, compatibility, assurance, and reliability. Gender was divided into two groups: males and females. Age was divided into four groups: 18-22 years, 23-35 years, 36-50 years, and 51 or older, which were coded numerically as 1, 2, 3, and 4. The dependent variable was customer loyalty.

This research investigated a broad framework under which a rhetorical theory of website design could be developed. The research design employed a quantitative method approach using 36 closed-ended questions, plus one open-ended question on the survey instrument, which scored on a 9-point Likert scale (1 = very strongly disagree, 5 = neither agree nor disagree, 9 = very strongly agree). The study used a sample of consumers who have previous experience with online products purchases. Data was collected in a period of four months from September to December of 2005. A total of 307 respondents (154 males and 153 females) entered their answers. The approximate time needed to completely the questionnaire was 5 to 7 minutes. This variety of respondents, who were invited to participate in this research, was primarily from U.S. Ages ranged from 18 to 75 years, with a mean age of 32.6 years. Collected data was analyzed by SPSS Windows Version 11.0. A total of five different statistical analyses were used in this research.

They were descriptive statistics, correlation analysis, independent-samples $t$ Test analysis, one-way ANOVA analysis, and multiple regression analysis.

The research process was preparation of the Web-based survey, running the survey, collecting the results, transferring the collected data into SPSS Software, and analysis of the results in SPSS Software. The significance of the overall model was evaluated by examined the R square values. Results of this survey indicated that logos, pathos, and ethos were three important visual aspects of successful websites. In addition, the empirical data validated rhetorical theory can certainly help online sellers to build websites that improve consumer loyalty.

**Research Findings**

This section provides the briefly answers for each research questions.

*Research Question 1*

What is the relationship between rhetorical elements (i.e., logos, pathos, and ethos) and customer loyalty in e-commerce websites?

Findings in question 1 reveal that consumer loyalty had a strong positive correlation to the three rhetorical elements (i.e., logos, pathos, and ethos) in e-commerce websites. Among three rhetorical elements, logos had the strongest relationship with consumer loyalty in this research, which was $r = .714$ and the relationship was statistically significant at the $p = < .01$ level. Visual design is the logical persuasive power when influencing online consumers to buy from virtual stores. A multiple regression analysis of all major independent variables resulted in an R square equal to .593 at the .01 level. Overall, the regression results support the inference of rhetorical elements (logos, pathos, and ethos) and consumer loyalty relationship. The findings underline the importance of rhetorical website design to drive consumer loyalty. That means classic rhetoric is a powerful strategy for dot-com sellers to adopt in order to persuade consumers to visit, stay with, and buy from the site repeatedly.

*Research Question 2*

What visual design elements and effectiveness constitute a persuasive model on a website?

Findings in question 2 reveal that eleven visual design elements (i.e., price, variety, product information, effort, playfulness, tangibility, empathy, recognizability, compatibility, assurance, and reliability) had a moderately strong effect on consumer loyalty in e-commerce websites. The R square was .628 with an overall significant at the .01 level, which made the findings statistically robust. That means these visual design elements and their effectiveness can really constitute a persuasive model on a website. Beta weight presents the level at which the independent variable is a predictor of the dependent variable. Altogether, the score of Beta weight showed that among eleven independent variables, ten visual design elements had positive statistically significant persuasive ability to consumer loyalty toward an e-commerce website. Only one visual design element (playfulness) had a negative influence on consumer loyalty. That means a playful website does not appear to have been a positive dominant factor in building consumer loyalty on e-commerce websites.

As to consumer loyalty, the strongest predictors form highest to lowest were: (1) Variety, (2) Recognizability, (3) Effort, (4) Price, (5) Product Information, (6) Reliability, (7) Assurance, (8) Tangibility, (9) Empathy, (10) Compatibility, and (11) Playfulness.

*Research Question 3*

Do males and females have different preferences in regard to visual design elements on a rhetorical website?

The independent-samples $t$ test can compare the means of two different groups (i.e., males and females). This analysis also can determine if the means of two groups' distributions differ significantly from each other. The final results show that among eleven visual design elements, there were no significant differences between males and females in nine design elements, since p > .05. The nine design elements were price, variety, product information, effort, tangibility, empathy, compatibility, assurance, and reliability. However, males and females differed significantly from each other in the visual elements of playfulness ($p = .006$) and recognizability ($p = .033$) on a rhetorical website. Males preferred the "fun" experiences than females in using the Web. Females were more concerned with strong corporate images and famous brand names than males in using the Web. This research indicates that if online dealers' target audiences are males, they should create a website that embraces more entertainment factors, in order to attract male audiences. On the other hand, if online companies established a successful corporate image on the Internet, it is easier to attract female audiences to purchase from them.

Generally speaking, online shoppers are very diverse. The results of this research have highlighted the importance of embracing a consumer-centered design approach when developing e-commerce strategies. In short, for companies that want to succeed on e-commerce, the most important thing is to design their website from consumers' perspective, to understand their customers' needs first, and utilize this information to design consumer-centered websites.

*Research Question 4*

Will different age groups have different preferences for rhetorical elements (i.e., logos, pathos, and ethos) on a website?

One-way ANOVA analysis was used to examine whether there are any statistical differences between diverse age groups in the rhetorical elements of a website. Post Hoc tests include a Scheffe test to identify between which groups differ significantly from each other. The final results show that there were no diverse preferences for the rhetorical element of logos among four age groups (18-22 years, 23-35 years, 36-50 years, and 51 or older) in this research. However, significant differences existed among the four groups for rhetorical elements of pathos and ethos. Age group1 (18-22 years) preferred emotional factors (i.e., playfulness, tangibility, and empathy) and trustworthy factors (i.e., recognizability, compatibility, assurance, and reliability) than other age groups in using a website. On the other hand, Group 4 (51 or older) paid less attention to the emotional factors and trustworthy factors than other age groups in using the Web.

The findings suggest that companies need to understand that online shoppers have diverse reasons to revisit the site. Actually, a website faces multiple end-users. Web designers should be mindful of those different end-users in mind at all times. By clearly knowing different age groups preferences, companies can select specific design elements that appeal to them. Consequently, this can generate additional sales and greater customer loyalty.

159

**Discussion**

This section presents the statistical results of each variable within the context of logos, pathos, and ethos. Consumer loyalty was the research dependent variable. The mean score of consumer loyalty was 7.45. Overall, consumer loyalty between the samples was moderately high. Figure 11 shows the histogram chart of consumer loyalty. The summary statistics for the rhetorical model was highly significant. The statistical findings reveal that participants felt this research had a right set of independent variables to predict the dependent variable.

Figure 11

*The Histogram Chart of Consumer Loyalty*

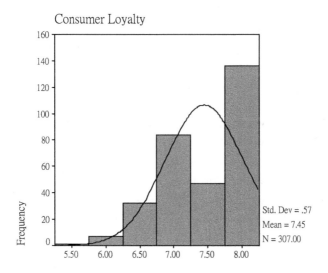

In this study, the researcher attempted to identify the salient factors that predict a consumer loyalty, using primary data from an online survey of Internet users in U.S. Among eleven rhetorical visual elements, the most persuasive factor was variety, and the least persuasive factor was playfulness. The individual results are discussed as below.

In rhetoric, logos is the rational and logical proofs. Website designs must appeal to reason and logic if online dealers want to sustain the long-term interest of their consumers. There were four salient factors under logos (price, variety, product information, and effort). After reviewing the Beta weight, it indicates that logos had the most unique effect on consumer loyalty, which was .525 at the .01 level of significance. In other words, the analysis shows that logos was the strongest predictor for consumer loyalty.

*Price*

Price had a positive standardized Beta weight with consumer loyalty. The score was .128 at the .01 level of significance. Based on the score of Beta weight, price was the fourth persuasive predictor in a rhetorical model on a website. Besides, price was the third salient factor in logos.

Cost savings is a potential benefit identified in the literature. The Internet puts comparison shopping at the consumers' fingertips than traditional stores. However, Winn and Beck (2002) mentioned that designers cannot decide the price for goods or service on the site, but price presentation can be used as a rhetorical tool to persuade consumers' price perception. Great price presentation is one of the convincing reasons for revisiting and building consumer loyalty to a site. For example, the site can provide attractive price options to consumers, such as: price comparisons with competitors, sales, discounts, and special offers. The goal is to design a price presentation on the website that can support consumers' price-conscious shopping habits, and facilitate consumers making purchase decisions quickly.

*Variety*

Variety had a positive standardized Beta weight with consumer loyalty. The score was .228 at the .01 level of significance. Based on the score of Beta weight, variety was the strongest persuasive predictor in a rhetorical model on a website. Besides, variety was the first salient factor in logos.

Variety refers to the product structure and display on the websites. Can online shoppers easily find their choices on the Web? Is there a number of items or a number of alternatives of the same items in stores? Is there a possibility for finding hard-to-find products when local offline store is out of stock? If customers cannot find the merchandise they desire in the stores, they might feel disappointed and never come back. On the other hand, consumers can have positive feelings with a website, if the site can present an accurate representation of products by exhibiting the breadth and depth of product variety. Results of this research provide support for Hoffman et al., (1995) contention that consumers benefit from the convenience of online purchasing from the growing variety of products sold on the Web. Consumers who have the specific products they desire to buy will see the Internet as an ideal place to find greater selection. Thus, the variety of products is an extremely vital feature to effect consumer intention to purchase online. Web designers should design a clear product structure and display on the sites to allow shoppers easy access to product categories without being confusing.

*Product information*

Product information had a positive standardized Beta weight with consumer loyalty. The score was .125 at the .01 level of significance. Based on the score of Beta weight, product information was the fifth persuasive predictor in a rhetorical model on a website. Besides, product information was the fourth salient factor in logos.

Before consumers buy a product, they need to collect a certain amount of information so they can feel comfortable the purchase. The Internet is an available place for consumers to gather information. Consumers can easily collect information without going out for different stores. By assisting consumers to access sufficient information, companies can keep their customers satisfied and establish good relationships. On the other hand, if consumers feel dissatisfied, they will leave the current site and never return. Carliner (2002) gave a suggestion for information design strategies from three different perspectives: (1) Physical design: can readers find the information they are looking for? (2) Cognitive design: how readers understand the information they are looking for? (3) Affective design: how do readers emotionally respond to the information? Consumers need to be able to understand the way information is presented on the site in order to make an effective decision. For example, companies could include a search box in every page and reference links to resources for their consumers to help them access information quickly. The findings of the research indicated that providing clear, up-to-date, accurate, sufficient, and easily accessible product information on the sites is one way to convince consumers to be loyal toward the sites over time.

*Effort*

Effort had a positive standardized Beta weight with consumer loyalty. The score was .195 at the .01 level of significance. Based on the score of Beta weight, effort was the third persuasive predictor in a rhetorical model on a website. Besides, effort was the second salient factor in logos.

Many websites have products and information that shoppers cannot find. Nielson (2000) mentioned that websites need to be concerned three basic questions for their end-users: (1) Where am I?, (2) Where have I been?, and (3) Where can I go? Create user-friendly navigational tools to ensure shoppers can access their desired information in few steps. An easy-of-use website need to ensure there are no difficulties to navigate on the Web, guarantee the information is accessible to all, and make sure the site is built on an intuitively systematic structure. For example, a website can have the direct devices like site maps, forward and backward buttons, headings, effective linking structures, table of contents, pages' numbers to minimize shoppers' effort. Fleming (1998) declared that Web designs need to be intuitive. This concept is strongly supported by Johnson-Sheehan and Baehr (2001). They believed that Web designers need to create an environment that allows consumers to save time and makes shopping easy. The findings in this research show that consumers can have optimistic attitudes toward a website if the site can offer intuitive navigation to allow them move freely around the site. Web designers should design sites' structure from consumers' perspectives, not purely from companies' structure. With such a design, consumers can feel that they are using the technology, not be used by the technology.

### *Pathos*

In rhetoric, pathos can be translated into emotional proofs. There were three salient factors under pathos (playfulness, tangibility, and empathy). After reviewing the Beta weight, it indicates that among three means of persuasion, pathos had the third unique effect on consumer loyalty, which was .047. However, it was not statistically significant since $p > .05$ ( $p = .261$).

*Playfulness*

Playfulness had a negative Beta weight. The score was -.082 at the .05 level of significance. Based on the score of Beta weight, playfulness was the least persuasive predictor in a rhetorical model on a website. Besides, playfulness was the third salient factor in pathos.

Playfulness refers to the entertainment value of websites in this research. A pleasant visual appeal can encourage shoppers to stay and revisit the sites. The goal is to present consumers a pleasant experience while navigating the website. The statistical results show playfulness had a negative Beta weight, which was significant at the .05 level. However, it is important to note that does not mean playfulness is not important in a rhetorical model of website. The data only imply that playfulness did not influence consumer loyalty as much as other design features.

The "fun" factor may be able to attract consumers to visit the site; however, enjoyment is not the key factor can increase the intention of making purchases on the site. Goal-oriented shoppers tend to focus their attention on things that can facilitate their ability to complete the online transactions quickly. Playful features may lead online buyers to spend more time on entertaining activities than shopping. Therefore, when designing an online shopping site, it is important to be aware that sometimes the role of playful media (e.g., games, jokes, and cartoons) might become a disturbing factor to purchasers from their final tasks.


*Tangibility*

Tangibility had a positive standardized Beta weight, which was .102 ( $p = .025$). It is statistically significant since $p = < .05$. Based on the score of Beta weight, tangibility was the eighth persuasive predictor in a rhetorical model on a website. Besides, tangibility was the first salient factor in pathos.

Fleming (1998) explained Web space as "virtual" because people cannot touch, smell, and taste in electronic environment. Many consumers still desire to touch merchandise before buying; thus, whether the website design can help consumers overcome the barriers of "no-touch feeling" should be an important issue to a successful online business. Usually, visual images can add better information content to Web pages. A picture, it is commonly said, is worth a thousand words. Colorful pictures can help shoppers browse online information more effectively and easily than texts. In other words, visual images not only can capture shoppers' attention on emotions but also can give a fresh dimension to the text-based Web page presented. Sites should include sensorially rich content that allow consumers to have a similar direct experience with a product in the virtual environment.

The research findings indicate that web designers can utilize visual images (e.g., colorful images, 3D virtual tours, and video films) and other multimedia features (e.g., audio effects) to create a "physical" dimension to online shopping, in order to compensate for the missing sensory experience on a website. However, Web designers need to notice that attach colorful images will not take too much time for shoppers to download a shopping page.

*Empathy*

Empathy had a positive standardized Beta weight, which was .100 at the .05 level of significance. Based on the score of Beta weight, empathy was the ninth persuasive predictor in a rhetorical model on a website. Besides, empathy was the second salient factor in pathos.

Empathy refers to personalization features of the site. Design for individual shopping styles, suggesting products, and services by personalizing the site. Newell (2000) illustrated that the Internet market is a one-to-one market; every consumer should be seen as a unique person who needs individual care. Companies need to learn each consumer's likes and dislikes, and ensure that they can fulfill shoppers' needs. The research findings suggest that in order to provide customers unique experiences, websites should offer personalized solutions to build specific relationship with consumers. This result reflected in Kasanoff, Peppers, and Rogers (2001) research, which stated that, "Personalization enables a business to match the right product or service to the right customer, for the right price, at the right time." (p.32). The strategy of providing personal

165

preferences of the customers on the sites allows companies to get much closer to consumers than traditional commerce.

## *Ethos*

In rhetoric, ethos is the credible proofs. There were four salient factors under ethos (recognizability, compatibility, assurance, and reliability). After reviewing the Beta weight, it indicates that among three means of persuasion, ethos had the second unique effect on consumer loyalty, which was .321 at the .01 level of significance.

*Recognizability*

Recognizability had a positive standardized Beta weight with consumer loyalty. The score was .195 at the .01 level of significance. Based on the score of Beta weight, recognizability was the second persuasive predictor in a rhetorical model on a website. Besides, recognizability was the first salient factor in ethos.

Many online vendors lack the physical embodiment of the companies' goods. Given the absence of physical exposure and contact, it is very difficult to identify whether an online seller is reputable on the Internet. For online consumers, a famous corporate image and brand name can increase their affirmative perception to a website, because a well-established brand name helps guarantee that the company is legitimate. In the high demanding online environment, how to build a strong corporate image is more crucial than ever. Marketers should consider this question before they enter the Internet business. The research results show that brand reputation is positively related to consumer loyalty on the websites. The more name brand recognition an e-shopping website can establish, the greater consumer loyalty will build.

*Compatibility*

Compatibility had a positive Beta weight with consumer loyalty. The score was .096 at the .05 level of significance. Based on the score of Beta weight, compatibility was the tenth persuasive predictor in a rhetorical model on a website. Besides, compatibility was the fourth salient factor in ethos.

One of particular uniqueness of the Internet marketing is that it consists of people who are connected to the Internet to share their common ideas, experiences, and interests

166

from different locations. Online merchants can create social-organizing efforts to bring consumers together. For example, firms can create a loyalty consumer club; consumers can receive a point every time they make a purchase or provide a useful suggestion. By encouraging consumers to share their suggestions and experiences with company and among themselves, website can help consumers feel that they belong to a group and willing to develop long-term relationship with the sites. In general, the on-line communication (i.e., newsgroups, electronic newsletters, bulletin boards, chat rooms, and discussion lists via the Internet) is a social-cultural relates to the experience of shopping.

The research findings suggest that consumers can have positive attitudes toward a website if the site has community building features on websites. However, online sellers need to notice that through electronic community, the power to transfer information is speedy and broadless. Online positive "word-of-mouth" communication may retain old consumers and bring more new customers. On the other hand, negative "word-of-mouth" communication could hurt companies' reputation badly. This means companies need to pay much attention on every contact with their consumers, and to ensure they can generate positive "word-of-mouth" referrals among the community members.

*Assurance*

Assurance had a positive standardized Beta weight, which was .111 at the .01 level of significance. Based on the score of Beta weight, assurance was the seventh persuasive predictor in a rhetorical model on a website. Besides, assurance was the third salient factor in ethos.

Assurance could be referred to as how much consumers perceived trustworthy information on the site. Online shoppers perceive risks when they purchase online because it is hard to tell which is a legitimate company or deceptive one. Cravotta (2000) advocated that security in transactions can give both consumers and vendors confidence. Privacy and security are main concern of the online shoppers. Much resistance has come from unsafe feelings. Companies need to be sensitive to consumers' need for privacy and security. Customers worry about the misuse of their personal information (i.e., third-party distribution and direct mailing). It is the firms' responsibility to carefully use the database of consumers in order to minimize consumers' perceived risk. Try not to invade the privacy by inappropriately sharing consumers' database with others. Security and privacy guarantees can symbolize a company's commitment to consumers. The research findings suggest that consumers can have positive attitudes toward a website, if the site clear states that all of the precautions have been taken by companies. By securing ordering process and providing an easy-to-read and unambiguous statement, companies can minimize consumers' risk perception online.

*Reliability*

Reliability had a positive standardized Beta weight, which was .117 at the .01 level of significance. Based on the score of Beta weight, reliability was the sixth persuasive predictor in a rhetorical model on a website. Besides, reliability was the second salient factor in ethos.

Reliability could be referred to customer service features on the sites. Superior customer service can enhance consumers' faith. websites need to offer some functional features which can enhance consumers' perception of reliability on their orders such as shipping dates, delivery time, tracking number, return police and procedures, e-mail address, toll-free telephone number, and 24-hour service. Consumers expect after-sales support 24 hours a day, 7 days a week, and 365 days per year. Therefore, excellent service can be a good opportunity to develop deeper and longer consumer relationship. Companies need to seize every opportunity to demonstrate quality service on the website to their customers. For example, Web designers should offer full contact information on sites and ensure all links are working. Firms need to make sure the contact information on the website can answer questions quickly and individually. These research findings suggest that the design features of reliability could influence shoppers' attitudes toward a site. Consumers can have positive attitudes toward a website, if the site can provide reliable services and multiple open communication channels.

**Limitations of the Research**

The research findings need to be considered with some limitations in mind. First of all, due to the dynamic nature of the Internet media, consumers' characteristics are likely to change with time. The researcher had analyzed the websites at one point in time in this research. Obviously similar studies at different times are likely to show different results. Basically, this research only provides a "snapshot" rather than long-term longitudinal study in Business-to-Consumer (B2C) Internet commerce.

Second, the sample has limitation. The study sample may not be representative of the population of Web shoppers because the sample is not derived from a random national sample of Internet users. Due to the nature of the sample, the generalizability of the finding is somewhat limited.

Third, in this research, the rhetorical set of independent variables accounts for a limited influence on the dependent variable (consumer loyalty). More independent variables need to be identified and specified in future research for a better understanding of Internet commerce.

Last, as the research context of the present study is Business-to-Consumer (B2C), the corresponding findings may not be applicable in other online trade models such as Business-to-Business (B2B), Government-to-Business (G2B), and Government-to-Consumer (G2C).

## Recommendations for Practical Implications

E-commerce is thriving. The future seems unlimited. However, the Internet is not a guaranteed path to success. There are lots of reasons that can lead to consumers' resistance when purchasing online. As online shopping is growing in popularity, there is clearly a need for more quantitatively driven empirical research in e-commerce area, with implemental recommendations for managers.

What do the findings of this research study mean for Business-to-consumer (B2C) e-commerce today? This research has some practical implications for website development. As with most endeavors, this research intended to identify the problems and find the best solutions for marketers. One of the major contributions of this research is to address the importance of rhetorical function of persuasion on the design elements of a website. This research reveals how to design persuasive sites through classic theories and systemic methods to convince consumers to purchase online. This research provides a crucial finding to facilitate the development of Internet commerce in persuasive discourse. From a marketing perspective, managers should create websites that fulfill needs of consumers by following this study's findings.

There are several practical implications for creating persuasive websites as follows:

1. In this research, a regression analysis of the set of independent variables (i.e., logos, pathos, and ethos) result in an $R^2 = .593$ with a significant at the .01 level. This finding implies that customer loyalty could increase if rhetorical concepts of logos, pathos, and ethos can present on websites. The research suggests that websites that can simultaneously operate on the basis of logos, pathos, and ethos have the best chances to win consumer loyalty.

2. Among three major rhetorical independent variables, logos had the most unique effect on consumer loyalty. In other words, logos was the strongest persuasive predictor for consumer loyalty. Therefore, if companies want to develop long-term relationship with their audiences, the most important strategy is to provide logical reasons (i.e., attractive price presentation, various choice products, clear and detailed product information, and intuitive navigation) to support their consumers in using the websites.

3. The results of the multiple regression analysis also showed that the eleven visual design elements (i.e., price, variety, product information, effort, playfulness, tangibility, empathy, recognizability, compatibility, assurance, and reliability) had a moderately strong effect on consumer loyalty in e-commerce websites. It means that increased the rhetorical visual design elements on websites can lead to greater intent to be loyal toward the sites. This finding illustrates that Web designers should understand that if they cannot increase the rhetorical elements on websites then they may lose customer loyalty.

4. The research results show that males and females differ significantly from each other in the visual elements of playfulness on a rhetorical website. Playfulness refers to the entertainment value of websites in this research. The research findings specify that males prefer the "fun" experiences to a great extent than females in using the Web. Therefore, if an online dealer's target audiences are males, he or she should consider creating a website not only to provide

information, but also to have more playful factors (i.e., games, jokes, and cartoons), in order to attract male visitors.

5. The final results confirm that there were significant differences between males and females in the visual elements of recognizability on a rhetorical website. The result implies that females are more concerned with strong corporate images and famous brand names than males in using the Web. Thus, a recognizable brand name can be an effective tool to win female consumers' trust easily when shopping online. If online companies' target audiences are females, it is important to establish strong online identifications in order to reduce female consumer anxiety from the indirect transaction. The research reveals that consumers need sufficient reasons to believe one specific website is truthful and reliable. Online dealers must carefully think what kind of design content can better engage their customers and increase their purchase intentions in the virtual mall. Once a target group has been identified, effective design strategies should be developed to attract the appropriate customer segments.

6. The Beta weight of the regression analysis showed that among the eleven independent variables, the strongest, most persuasive predictor of consumer loyalty was variety. Customers who have the specific products they desire to buy will see the Internet as an ideal place to find greater selection. If consumers cannot find the merchandise they desire in the on-line stores, they might feel disappointed and never come back. The researcher suggests that Web designers should design a clear product structure and display on the sites to allow shoppers to easily find their choices. For example, online dealers should build clear and ease-to-use references categories to help customers gain access to their desired products without confusion.

7. Among the eleven independent variables, the weakest persuasive predictor of consumer loyalty was playfulness. Playfulness had a negative Beta weight, which was significant at the .05 level. The result implies that playfulness did not influence consumer loyalty as much as other design features. That means playful features (e.g., games, jokes, and cartoons) are not the key factor can increase consumers' purchase intention on the site. Undeniably, many online shoppers are

171

goal-focused consumers. Goal-oriented shoppers desire to purchase what they want quickly without distraction. Therefore, when designing an online shopping site, it is important to efficiently balance the role of playful media on the sites.

8. There were diverse preferences existed among the four age groups for rhetorical elements of pathos in this research. Age group1 (18-22 years) paid more attention to the emotional factors than other age groups. The result implies that young people enjoy games, cartoons, jokes, colorful images, video films, 3D virtual tour, audio effects, and personalization features on the sites, to a greater extent than other age groups. This result can help us understand that websites, which have the rhetorical elements of pathos, can launch their Internet commerce more easily with young audiences.

9. There were diverse preferences for the rhetorical element of ethos among four age groups in this research. Age group1 (18-22 years) paid most attention to the trustworthy features (i.e., recognizability, compatibility, assurance, and reliability) that the website established. Prior studies indicated that younger age groups use computers and the Internet widely for many of their daily activities (Pastore, 2001). Young shoppers have more experience in purchasing online than other age group. Given the lack of physical exposure and contact, they realize there are many deceptive companies on the Internet; thus, they are more cautious with secure online shopping factors. The finding appears that young consumers prefer the idea of strong corporate images, famous brand names, bulletin boards, chat rooms, personal privacy and security, and high-quality consumer service when shopping online.

To summarize, in the online environment, consumers are more active than in traditional media. When designing a website, companies need to employ rhetorical tools to convince consumers to visit their site repeatedly. Web developers should shape the Web style for their specific consumers' needs. In other words, rhetorical website designs must put consumers at the center of all Web development decisions. Web designers should consider how to approach consumers' experiences, expectations, values, and attitudes when they think about the content of website design. When a website can fully deliver a superior online shopping experience, it could be a win-win situation for both online dealers and shoppers.

## Recommendations for Future Research

To further our understanding of the effects of rhetorical tools in the Internet, future work may be done at both a pedagogical and an operational level. This research provides many opportunities for future research as follows:

1. Additional empirical studies can be conducted across national borders to compare the study cross-cultural differences between countries. Such replication will help us understand if geographic influences play a specific role on borderless online market.

2. The measurement created for this research should undergo future refinement. First, more research needs to be done on refining the measures used in this research. Similar findings would provide additional support for the instrument. In addition, more questions could be added into the questionnaire in order to improve reliability and validity of the survey instrument.

3. Future research could focus on developing additional rhetorical design items to fully study website. Also, a comprehensive design guideline which is related to rhetorical design features needs to be developed. The academic community could employ such a details framework for a comparison of the results of Web studies with different categories of sites or user groups.

4. Since the Internet is a highly dynamic medium, future research should also consider the need for longitudinal research to provide more feasible and powerful variables that persuade online consumers' purchasing decisions over time.

## Conclusions

The Internet has a profound impact on global market; however, it also raises many unsolved questions to marketers. This research is related with one of the most important topics of business, which is a great effort to achieve consumer loyalty in virtual environment. Actually, consumer loyalty has been widely discussed for decades but marketing environments have changed dramatically since the development of the Internet.

Prior studies that addressed consumer loyalty in traditional business settings may be not appropriate in a new dimension of electronic environment. Besides, when formulating the Internet strategies, many Web-based companies lean to focus on the technological aspect rather than from customers' perspective of website design. Only a few empirical-based studies investigating rhetorical Web design and its relationship to online loyalty have been published to date. In the virtual mall, website s are the bridges between companies and consumers. It is important to look at the relationship between website design and consumer loyalty and find design effects on electronic shopping.

This study implemented a rhetorical approach to understanding consumer loyalty in the Internet commerce. The researcher expected that a rhetorical approach can help in formulating answers to existing questions. Therefore, this research measured a theoretical framework of how visual design variables considered contributors to rhetorical website s might predict consumer loyalty in Business-to-consumer (B2C) Internet context. This research has answered four research questions. (1)What is the relationship between rhetorical elements (i.e., logos, pathos, and ethos) and customer loyalty in e-commerce websites? (2) What visual design elements and effectiveness constitute a persuasive model on a website? (3) Do males and females have different preferences in regard to visual design elements on a rhetorical website? (4) Will different age groups have different preferences for rhetorical elements (i.e., logos, pathos, and ethos) on a website? Four questions have been examined with different statistical analyses, adding to the future to the literature of the persuasive power of rhetorical website design on consumer loyalty in Business-to-Consumer (B2C) Internet commerce. To a great extent, this research not only gave a solid Web knowledge base to current Internet marketing but also allows managers to use such a knowledge base in practice.

Taken over, the research found that increased the rhetorical elements on websites will lead to greater intent to be loyal toward the site. These findings support the initial assumption of the research, which was the rhetorical design elements of a website can positively affect consumers' reaction toward a site. In addition, the researcher expected that consumers who perceived sites high in rhetoric would develop optimistic attitudes that endured over time. The empirical data validated rhetorical theory can help online sellers to build websites that improve consumer loyalty.

To ensure the success of online businesses, there are several considerations for creating persuasive websites. First, persuasive websites must consider the needs and preferences of their audience. Second, persuasive websites should employ three rhetorical principles in their appearances. Third, customer loyalty could increase if salient visual features were present on websites. Fourth, these rhetorical features are interrelated with each other although they are different. Lastly, effective websites with design features that facilitate consumer loyalty are likely to represent the future of electronic marketing. These findings will help online marketers and Web designers to create the most persuasive site environment for online shoppers.

Over 2,000 years ago, Aristotle gave the concept of three means of persuasion within the context of interpersonal communication. Nowadays, rhetorical design on the Web as a field is developing. Rhetoric means here is not purely the principles of speech or verbal discourse but a visual context. Rhetorical design is concerned with modification of the consumer's attitude toward the site. In the online context, visual persuasion of design elements has the significant effect to influence consumers' decision-making. A rhetorical website can combine theory with application in a way satisfying both to the consumers and to the marketers.

In summary, the Internet brings dramatic improvements to economic efficiency. Marketers need to realize that it is very important for them to develop appropriate strategies in order to attract and keep consumers at their sites, satisfied that their search is over. The research offers suggestions on using rhetorical tools to create a win-win situation for companies. The rhetorical principle can give a new vitality to a website. The more rhetorical elements that online sellers can offer through the visual display of websites, the more interested the consumers will be in purchasing on the sites. Web page designers need to understand what consumers expect from sites, and take this into account and display the most persuasive design elements on the screen to consumers. As more consumers turn to online shopping, firms need to prepare a perfect shopping environment to convince consumers to revisit, repeat purchase, and engage in "word-of-mouth" referrals to them. Ultimately, a persuasive website design will be the glue to hold consumers and marketers together over time.

## REFERENCES

Abramson, J. & Hollingshead, C. (1998). Marketing on the Internet: providing consumer satisfaction. *Journal of Internet Marketing, 1,* Retrieved March 1, 2004, from http://www.arraydev.com/commerce/JIM/9802-01.htm.

Albee Cibops Smart Web business.com (2002). Number of U.S. small businesses connected to the Internet. Retrieved Jun 16, 2003, from http://www.smartwebbusiness.com/netinfo/smallbizsoaring.htm

Anderson, T., & Kanuka, H. (2003). *e-Research: methods, strategies, and issues.* Boston, MA: Pearson education, Inc.

Andrisani, D., Gaal, A. V., Gillette, D., & Steward, S. (2001). Making the most of interactivity online. *Technical Communication, 48,* 309-323, Washington, Aug 2001. Retrieved April 17, 2002, from the ProQuest database.

Anonymous (2001). Internet works. *Signal, 55,* 12, Falls Church, Feb 2001. Retrieved March 22, 2002, from the ProQuest database.

AT & T Technology (1995). Where it came from, how it grew. *AT & T Technology, 10,* Autumn 1995. Retrieved July 20, 2003, from www.texshare.edu.

Babbie, E. (1990). Survey *research methods* (2nd ed.). Belmont, CA: Wadsworth.

Babbie, E. (2001). *The practice of social research* (9th ed.). Belmont, CA: Wadsworth.

Baker, T. L. (1999). *Doing social research* (3rd ed.). New York: McGraw-Hill College.

Baumgardt, M. (2002). *Adobe Photoshop 7 Web Design with GoLive 6.* Berkeley, CA: Adobe Press.

Bell, J., & Castagna, R. (1997). If you build it, they will come. *Windows magazine, 8,* 195-198, July, 1997.

Benjamin, R., & Wigand, R. (1995). Electronic markets and virtual value chains on the information superhighway. *Sloan Management Review,* 62-67.

Berry, D. (2003). CRM for the small to medium enterprise - king-sized CRM on a bite-sized budget. *Customer Interaction Solutions, 21,* 56-59. May 2003. Retrieved Jun 2, 2003, from the ProQuest database.

Berry, L. L. (1995). Relationship marketing of services growing interest, emerging perspective. *Journal of the Academy of Marketing Science. 23,* 236-245, Fall 1995.

Bishop, W. (1998). *Strategic Marketing for the digital age.* Chicago, IL: American

Marketing Association.

Black, T. R. (1999). *Doing quantitative research in the social sciences: An integrated approach to research design, measurement and statistics.* Thousand Oaks, CA: Sage Publication, Inc.

Bolter, J. D. (1991). *Writing space: the computer, hypertext, and the history of writing.* New York: Lawrence Erlbaum Associates, Inc.

Braddock, R. S. (2001). The Internet: the novel. *Financial Analysts Journal, 57,* 17-19, Charlottesville, Sep/Oct 2001. Retrieved December 15, 2002, from the ProQuest database.

Brennan, R. (1999). Relationship management in the automotive industry. *International Journal of Customer Relationship Management.* April 1999.

Bright, D. (1998). Conran Restaurants – Meeting customer expectations. *International Journal of Customer Relationship Management.* June/July 1998.

Brown, E. (2002). eBay: how can a dot-com be this hot? *Fortune.* Retrieved Jun 16, 2003, from Fortune website:
http://www.fortune.com/fortune/technology/articles/0,15114,370988,00.html

Brown, G. H. (1953). Brand loyalty- fact or fiction? *Advertising Age,* Jun 1953.

Bunnell, D. & Richard, L. (2000). *The eBay phenomenon: business secrets behind the world's hottest Internet company.* New York: John Wiley & Sons, Inc.

Bulkely, W. M. & Carlton, J. (2000). E-tail gets derailed: how Web upstarts misjudged the game. *The Wall Street Journal.* April 2000. Retrieved August 2, 2003, from the ProQuest database.

Burgess, T. F. (2001). A general introduction to the design of questionnaires for survey research. Retrieved April 18, 2003, from University of Leeds Information System Services website:
http:// www.leeds.ac.uk/iss/documentation/top/top2.pdf

Cai, Y. (2001). Design strategies for global products. *Design Management Journal, 12,* 59-64, Boston, Fall 2001. Retrieved March 22, 2004, from the ProQuest database.

Capodagli, B., & Jackson, L (2001). *Leading at the speed of change: using new economy rules to invigorate old economy companies.* NJ: McGraw-Hill.

Carliner, S. (2002). Designing better documents. *Information Management Journal, 36,*

42-51, Prairie Village, Sep/Oct 2002. Retrieved December 8, 2003, from the ProQuest database.

Carroll, J., & Brodhead, R. (2001). *Selling online: how to become a successful E-commerce merchant.* Chicago, IL: Dearborn Trade, a Kaplan Professional Company.

Cato, J. (2001). *User-centered Web design.* London: Addison-Wesley.

Christopher, J. & McKenzie, G. (2003). *Mining online gold with an offline shovel.* Los Angeles, CA: Mastermind.

Colby, K. L. (2002). E-Commerce: a growing presence. *Alaska Business Monthly, 18,* 28, Anchorage, Nov 2001. Retrieved March 22, 2003, from the ProQuest database.

Commerce Net. (1999). Internet population. Retrieved January 18, 2003, from Commerce Net website: http://www.commerce.net/research/starts/wwwpop.html.

Commerce Net. (2001). World wide Internet population. Retrieved January 18, 2003, from Commerce Net website:

http://www.commerce.net/research/starts/wwstats.html.

Coney, M. B., & Steehouder, M. (2000). Role playing on the Web: Guidelines for designing and evaluating personas online. *Technical Communication, 3,* 327-340, Washington, Aug 2000. Retrieved March 22, 2003, from the ProQuest database.

Cordy, E. D. (2003). The legal regulation of e-commerce transactions. *Journal of American Academy of Business, 2,* 400-407, Cambridge, Hollywood, Mar 2003. Retrieved March 2, 2004, from the ProQuest database.

Covino, W. A., & Jolliffe, D. A. (1995). *Rhetoric: concepts, definitions, boundaries.* Boston: Allyn and Bacon.

Coyle, J. R., & Thorson, E. (2001). The effects of progressive levels of interactivity and vividness in Web marketing sites. *Journal of Advertising, 3,* 65-77, Provo, Fall 2001. Retrieved April 18, 2003, from the ProQuest database.

Cravotta, N. (2000). Securing the wireless World Wide Web. *EDN, 45,* 89-100, Boston, Aug 17, 2000. Retrieved December 15, 2002, from the ProQuest database.

Creativeflavor.com. (2003). Effective e-commerce site design. Retrieved May 22, 2003, from Creativeflavor.com website:

http://www.creativeflavor.com/WP_Ecommerce.asp.

Cremel, N. (2001). A Little History of the World Wide Web: from 1960s to 1995

Retrieved April 18, 2002, from CERN website:

http://ref.cern.ch/CERN/CNL/2001/001/www-history/

Culman, M. J. (1995). Consumer awareness of name removal procedures: implications for direct marketing. *Journal of Direct Marketing*, *9*, 10-19, Spring 1995.

CustomerCentric (2002). Leveraging predictive analytics in marketing campaigns. Retrieved December 4, 2003, from SPSS Inc. website: http://www.spss.com/customercentric

Cutler, M., & Sterne, J. (2001). E-metrics: business metrics for the new economy. Retrieved December 15, 2002, from Target Marketing website: http://www.targeting.com/emetrics.pdf

Deck, S. (2001). What is CRM? Retrieved 23 Jun, 2003, from Darwinmag.com website: http://www.darwinmag.com/learn/curve/column.html?ArticleID=104

Dick, A. S., & Basu, K. (1994). Customer loyalty: toward an integrated conceptual framework. *Journal of Academy of Marketing Science*, *22*, 99-113.

Dillman, D. A. (2000). *Mail and Internet surveys: The tailored design method* (2nd ed.). New York: John Wiley & Son, Inc.

Doney, P. M., & Cannon, J. P. (1997). An examination of the nature of trust in buyer-seller relationship. *Journal of Marketing*, *61*, 35-51, April 1997.

Dormann, C. (1997). Persuasive Interface: Designing for the WWW. *International Professional Communication Conference (IEEE)*. 345-354, Salt Lake, April 1997. Retrieved Jun 4, 2003, from http://www-faculty.cs.uiuc.edu/~bpbailey/publications/hfweb-2001.pdf

Drapkin, M., Lowy, J. & Marovitz, D. (2001). *Three Clicks Away: Advice from the Trenches of eCommerce*. New York: John Wiley.

Dugan, S. M. (2000). The best loyalty program for your website may be better customer service. *InfoWorld*. *22*, 15, May 2000. Retrieved 23 February, 2004, from InfoWorld website: http://archive.infoworld.com/articles/op/xml/00/05/15/000515opprophet.xml

Dunt, E. S., & Harper, I. R. (2002). E-commerce and the Australian economy. *Economic Record*, *78*, 327-342, East Ivanhoe, Sep 2002. Retrieved Jun 4, 2004, from the ProQuest database.

Easley, R. W. (2002). Virtual communities…the power of word-of-mouth transmission via the Internet. *Journal of Internet Marketing, 2* (1), March 2002. Retrieved 23 Jun, 2003, from Journal of Internet Marketing website: http://www.arraydev.com/commerce/jim/0203-04.htm

Ehses, H. H. (1989). Representing machete: a case study in visual rhetoric. *In Design Discourse.* London: Chicago University Press.

ePaynews. com. (2002). eCommerce still stunted by security fears. Retrieved Jun 4, 2003, from the ePayments Resource Center website: http://www.cardinalcommerce.com/articles/October_2002/eCommerce%20Stil l%20Stunted%20By%20Security%20Fears.htm.

Farkas, D. K., & Farkas, J. B. (2000). Guidelines for designing web navigation. *Technical Communication, 3,* 341-358, Washington, Aug 2000. Retrieved April 20, 2002, from the ProQuest database.

Finnie, W., & Randall, R. M. (2002). Loyalty as a philosophy and strategy: an interview with Frederick F. Reichheld. *Strategy & Leadership. 30,* 25-31, Chicago. Retrieved Jun 26, 2003, from the ProQuest database.

Fiore, F. (2000). *e-Marketing Strategies.* Chicago: Que Publishers.

Fleming, J. (1998). *Web navigation: designing the user experience.* Sebastopol, CA: O'Reilly & Associations, Inc.

Forrester Research. (2001). Forrester Research reports on e-business. Retrieved January 25, 2002, from Forrester Research website: http://www.napm.org/ISMReport/Forrester/index.cfm .

Forrester Research. (2001). Worldwide Internet population statistics. Retrieved January 25, 2002, from Forrester Research website: http://www.forrester.com/Home/standard/0,1184,114,00.html

Foster, J., Emberton, D. J., & Bauer, P. (2001). *Photoshop 6 Web Magic.* Indianapolis: IN: New Riders Publishing.

Fry, A., Paul, D. (1995). *How to publish on the Internet: A comprehensive step-by-step guide to creative expression on the World Wide Web.* New York: Warner Books.

Gall, M. D., Borg, W. R., & Gall, J. P. (1996). *Educational research: An introduction* (6th ed.). White Plains, New York: Longman Publishers.

Garrett, J. J. (2002). *The elements of user experience: user-centered design for the Web.* New York: New Riders.

George, D. & Mallery, P. (2001). *SPSS for Windows step by step: a simple guide and reference* (3rd ed.). Needham Heights, NJ: Allyn & Bacon.

Geyskens, I. J., Steenkamp, L. K., Scheer, & Kumar, N. (1996). The effects of trust and Interdependence on relationship commitment: a trans-Atlantic-study. *International Journal of Research in Marketing,* 13, 303-317, 1996.

Giddens, A. (2000). *The Third Way: The Renewal of Social Democracy.* Chicago: Polity Press.

Grant, T. L. (1999). Internet business models update: who will win? Retrieved January 18, 2003, from Commerce Net website: http://www.commerce.net/research/ebusiness-strategies/1999/ 99_24_r.html

Grant Thornton.com (2003). Capital markets. Retrieved March 1, 2003, from Grant Thornton website: http://www.grantthornton.com/content/10312.asp

Gray, M. (1995). Comprehensive list of sites. Retrieved March 1, 2003, from http://www.mit.edu/people/mkgray/net/

Greenberg, C. J. (1998). Beyond HTML! *Information Outlook, 11,* 26-30, Washington, Nov 1998. Retrieved April 22, 2003, from the ProQuest database.

Gromov, G. (1995). Internet pre-history: Ancient roads of telecommunications and computers. Retrieved April 18, 2002, from Net Valley website: http://www.netvalley.com/intval_intr.html.

Gromov, G. R. (2001). The roads and crossroads of Internet History. Retrieved April 18, 2001, from Net Valley website: http://www.netvalley.com/intvalstat.html

Gutterman, A., Brown. R., & Stanislaw, J. (2000). *Doing business on the Internet.* Orlando, FL: Harcourt, Inc.

Hall, R.E. (2001). *Digital dealing: how e-markets are transforming the economy.* New York: W.W. Norton & Company, Inc.

Hamman, R. (1998). History of the Internet, WWW, IRC, and MUDs. Retrieved April 18, 2002, from http://www.socio.demon.co.uk/history.html.

Hampton, R. E. (1990). The rhetorical and metaphorical nature of graphics and visual schemata. *Rhetoric Society quarterly, 20,* 347-356, Fall 1990. Retrieved April 20,

2003, from the ProQuest database.

Haig, M. (2001). *The e-marketing handbook: an indispensable guide to marketing.* Dover, London: British Library.

Harrison-Walker, L. J. (2002). If you build it, will they come? Barriers to international e-marketing. *Journal of Marketing Theory and Practice, 10,* 12-21, Statesboro, Spring 2002. Retrieved December 1, 2003, from the ProQuest database.

Heuberger, A. (2001). Manage your global WWW brand. *World Trade. 14,* 56-60, Tory, Nov 2001. Retrieved February 7, 2002, from the ProQuest database.

High-Tech Dictionary (2003). Retrieved Jun 5, 2003, from High-Tech dictionary Web site:

http://www.computeruser.com/resources/dictionary/definition.html?lookup=6318.

Hirschman, E. C., & Thompson, C. (1997). Why media matter: toward a richer understanding of consumers' relationships with advertising and mass media. *The Journal of Advertising, 26,* Spring 1997. Retrieved August 5, 2003, from the Journal of Advertising website: http://sjmc.cla.umn.edu/joa/26.1.97.html

Hijazi, N. (2000). Online purchasing habits of Britons. *Research Analyst.* Retrieved Jun 5, 2003, from Commerce website:

http://www.commerce.net/research/ebusiness-reports/2000/43_20_r.html.

Hill, K. (2002). Survey: high customer expectations trump low satisfaction. Retrieved Jun 15, 2003, from Ecommerce Times website:

http://www.ecommercetimes.com/perl/story/16619.html

Hoffman, D. L., Novak, T. P., & Peralta, M. (1999). Building customer trust in online environment: the case for information privacy. *Communications of ACM, 42,* 80-85, April 1999. Retrieved Jun 15, 2003, from eLab website: http://elab.vanderbilt.edu/research/papers/html/manuscripts/cacm.privacy98/cacm. privacy98.htm

Hoffman, D. L., Thomas, P. N., & Chatterjee, P. (1995). Commercial scenarios for the Web: opportunities and challenges. *Journal of Computer- Mediated Communications. 1,* 1-21. Retrieved November 18, 2002, from JCMC website: http://www.ascusc.org/jcmc/vol1/issue3/hoffman.html.

Houser, R. (2001). Why we should archive, share, and analyze information about users.

*Technical Communication*, 2, 176-181, Washington, May 2001. Retrieved April 20, 2004, from the ProQuest database.

Hovland, C. I., Janis, I, L, & Kelley, H. H. (1953). Communication and persuasion. New Haven, CT: Yale University Press.

Howard, T. W. (1997). *A rhetoric of electronic communities*. Greenwich, CT: Ablex.

Huizingh, E. (2000). The content and design of website s: an empirical study. *Information and Management, 37*, 123-134, 2000.

Hwang, S. L. (2000). An Internet start-up gets almost everything right-except timing. *The Wall Street Journal*, April 2000. Retrieved October 10, 2003, from the ProQuest database.

ISC. (2008). ISC Internet Domain Suvey. Retrieved Setember 9, 2008, from Internet Systems Consortium, Inc. website: http://www.isc.org/index.pl

Isidro, B. M. (2002). 10 power steps to small business success. Retrieved Jun 4, 2003, from KataueyDesignWorks website: http://www.katsueydesignworks.com/ebizarticle1.htm

Jacoby, J., & Chestnut. R. W. (1978). *Brand loyalty: measurement and management*. New York: John Wiley & Sons.

Jarvenpaa, S., & Todd, P. (1996). Consumer reactions to electronic shopping on the World Wide Web. *International Journal of Electronic Commerce, 1*, 59-88. Retrieved November 18, 2003, from the ProQuest database.

Joel, P. (1998). Riding the Net's success. *Business Record, 15*, 18, Des Moines, Dec 1998. Retrieved July 8, 2002, from the ProQuest database.

Johnson, R. R. (1998). *User-centered technology: a rhetorical theory for computers and other mundane artifacts*. Albany, New York: State University of New York Press.

Johnson-Sheehan, R., & Baehr, C. (2001). Visual-spatial thinking in hypertexts. *Technical Communication, 48*, 22-30, Washington, Feb 2001. Retrieved Oct 8, 2003, from the ProQuest database.

Joyce, R. (2001). Digitization, the Internet, and electronic commerce. *Futurics, 25*, 95-98, St. Paul, Fall 2001. Retrieved January 13, 2003, from the ProQuest database.

Juran, J. M., & Gryna, F. M. (1970). *Quality planning and analysis: from product development through usage*. New York: McGraw-Hill.

Kasanoff, B., Peppers. D., & Rogers, M. (2002). *Making it personal: how to profit from personalization without invading privacy.* MA: Perseus Publishing.

Kalakota, R., & Whinston, A. B. (1997). *Electronic Commerce: A manager's guide.* MA: Addison- Wseley Reading.

Kalin, S. (1999). The Worldlier Wider Web. *CIO Web Business Magazine*, March 1999. Retrieved August 30, 2002, from http://www2.cio.com/archive/printer.cfm?URL=webbusiness/030199 axes print.cfm.

Keeney, R. (1999). The value of Internet commerce to the customer. *Management Science. 45*, 533-542, April 1999. Retrieved July 3, 2003, from http://coof.ba.ttu.edu/zlin/readings/Keenry-EC-value-MS.pdf

Kennedy, G. A. (1991). *Aristotle on rhetoric: a theory of civic discourse.* New York: Oxford University Press.

Kevin, H. (1996). Establishing a presence on the World Wide Web: A rhetorical approach. *Technical Communication, 43*, 376-387, Washington, Nov 1996. Retrieved Nov 18, 2002, from the ProQuest database.

Kimery, K. M., & McCord, M. (2002). Third-party assurance: mapping the road to trust in e-retailing. *JITTA: Journal of Information Technology Theory and Application. 4*, 63-82, Hong Kong. Retrieved Nov 18, 2003, from the ProQuest database.

Kirkby, A. (2001). Communication theory. *SPC, Soap, Perfumery, and Cosmetics. 74*, 44-48, Dartford, Mar 2001. Retrieved February 9, 2002, from the ProQuest database.

Koehler, W. (1999). Digital libraries and World Wide website s and page persistence. *Information Research, 4*, July 1999. Retrieved Jun 10, 2003, from http://informationr.net/ir/4-4/paper60.html

KPMG (2001). Loyalty 4 profits: how do retailers create loyalty 4 profits? Retrieved Jun 30, 2003, from KPMG International website: http://www.kpmg.co.uk/kpmg/uk/image/loyalty fact.pdf

LaBarbera, P. A., & Mazursky, D. (1983). A longitudinal assessment of consumer satisfaction/dissatisfaction: a dynamic aspect of cognitive process. *Journal of Marketing Research. 393-404*, Nov 1983.

Laffoon, E. A. (1998). Rhetoric and the arts of design. *Argumentation and Advocacy, 35*, 89-93, Fall 1998. Retrieved Nov 18, 2002, from the ProQuest database.

Lamb, B. (1998). Rhetoric. *English Journal. 87*, 108-109, Urbana, Jan 1998. Retrieved Nov 18, 2002, from the ProQuest database.

Larson, R., & Farber, B. (2000). *Elementary Statistics: picturing the world.* Upper Saddle River, NJ: Prentice Hall, Inc.

Leebaert, D. (1998). *The future of the electronic marketing.* Cambridge, London: MIT Press.

Liu, C., Arnett, K. (2000). Exploring the factors associated with website success in the context of electronic commerce. *Information and Management. 38*, 23-33, October 2000.

Lynch, P.D., Kent, R.J., Gillete, D., & Srinivasan, S.S. (2001). The global Internet shopper: Evidence from shopping tasks in twelve countries. *Journal of Advertising Research, 2*, 15-23, Jun 2001. Retrieved April 23, 2002, from the ProQuest.

Lynch, P. J., & Horton, S. (1999). *Web Style Guide: basic design principles for creating Web sites.* Boston: Yale University Press.

MacKenzie, A. (1997). *The time trap: the classic book on time management* (3rd ed.). New York: American Management Association.

MacQuillin, R. (2003). Auto-replenish for customer loyalty. Retrieved Jun 30, 2003, from McQuillin & Associates website: http://www.makelifeeasy.com/Resources/Merchant_Partnering.asp?T=CL

Malone, T. W., Yates, J., & Benjamin, R. I. (1989). The logic of electronic markets. *Harvard Business Review*, 166-172.

Mann, C. L. (2002). Achieving the benefits of connectivity and global e-commerce. Retrieved February 2, 2003, from Institute for International Economics website: http://www.iie.com/publications/papers/mann0702.pdf

Marcus, A. (1993). Human communications issues in advanced user interfaces. *Communications of the ACM, 26*, 101-109.

Marcus, G., & Fischer, M. (1986). *Anthropology as cultural critique: an experimental moment in the human sciences.* Chicago: University of Chicago.

May, P. (2000). *The business of ecommerce: from corporate strategy to technology.*

Cambridge: Cambridge University.

McKnight, D. H., Cummings, L. L., & Chervany, N. L. (1998). Initial trust formation in new organizational relationships. *Academy of Management Review, 23*, 473-490.

Merriam-Webster Dictionary. (2003). Retrieved Jun 5, 2003, from Merriam-Webster website: http://www.merriam-webster.com/cgi-bin/dictionary?va=acumens .

Miccrosoft. com. (2003). Business Benefits: Microsoft solutions for Internet business. January 15. Retrieved Jun 9, 2003, from http://www.microsoft.com/solutions/MSIB/evaluation/benefits/default.asp

Michael, C. (2000). *Smart things to know about E-commerce.* Oxford: Capstone Publishing Ltd.

Mitchell, A. S. (2002). Do you really want to understand your customer? *Journal of Consumer Behaviour. 2*, 71-79, London, Sep 2002. Retrieved Jun 26, 2003, from the ProQuest database.

Mountford, S. J. (1990). Tools and techniques for creative design. *The art of human-computer interface design.* MA: Addison-Wesley.

Mortensen, K. W. (2003). How to create instant influence: what you want, when you want, and win friends for life. Retrieved Jun 27, 2003, from Multiple Streams of Income website: http://www.robertgallen.com/mag_per.htm

Mountain Media. (2003). eCommerce solutions: shopping cart. Retrieved May 18, 2003, from Mountain Media website: http://www.mountainmedia.com/index.cfm?a=12

Network Wizards. (1996). The growth of Internet hosts and domains. Retrieved April 18, 2003, from Network Wizards website: http://www.isc.org/ds/WWW-9607/report.html

Newell, F. (2000). *Loyalty.com: customer relationship management in the new era of Internet Marketing.* New York: McGraw-Hill.

Nielson, J. (2000). *Design Web usability: the practice of simplicity.* New York: New Riders

Novak, T. P., Hoffman, D.L., & Yung, Y. (1999). Measuring the customer experience in online environments: a structural modeling approach. *Marking Science, 19*, 22-44, Winter 1999. Retrieved April 22, 2003, from http://pubsonline.informs.org/main/pdfstore/af8f4ec876_abstract.pdf

Oliver, R. L. (1999). Whence consumer loyalty? *Journal of Marketing, 63* (Special
Issue), 33-44, Feb 1999.

Page, K. A. (2002). *Macromedia Dreamweaver MX: training from the source.*
Berkeley, CA: Macromedia Press.

Pal, N., & Ray, M. (2001). *Pushing the digital frontier: insights into the changing
landscape of e-business.* New York: American Management Association.

Pandia (2001). On the size of the World Wide Web. Retrieved April 18, 2003, from
Pandia website: http://www.pandia.com/sw-2001/57-websize.html

Parsons, A., Zeisser, M., & Waitman, R. (1998). Organizing today for the digital
marketing of tomorrow. *Journal of Interactive Marketing.* 12, 31-46, New York,
Winter 1998.

Pastore, M (2001). Young Internet users prefer e-browsing to e-commerce. Retrieved
April 9, 2004, from ClickZ Network website:
http://www.clickz.com/stats/big_picture/applications/article.php/707631

Patrick, J. & Lynch, S. H. (1997). *Web style guide: Yale style manual.* (2nd ed.).
Retrieved March 18, 2002, from Yale Center website:
http://info.med.yale.edu/caim/manual/

Payne, A., & Rickard. J. (1997). Relationship marketing, consumer retention and firm
profitability. *Cranfield School of Management*, 283-285, Bedford, UK. August
1997.

Peeples, D. K. (2002). Instilling consumer confidence in e-commerce. *S. A. M.
Advanced Management Journal, 67*, 26-31, Cincinnati, Autumn 2002. Retrieved
on December 15, 2003, from the ProQuest database.

Peterson, R. A., Balasubramanian, S., & Bronnenberg, B. J. (1997). Exploring the
implications of the Internet for consumer marketing. *Journal of the Academy of
Marketing Science, 25*, 329-346.

Plant, R. (2000). *eCommerce formulation of strategy.* Upper Saddle River, NJ: Prentice
Hall PTR.

Podlogar, M. (1998). Consumer reactions to electronic shopping on the Internet. Jun
1998. Retrieved on April 15, 2002, from

http://ecom.fov.uni-mb.si/mateja/clanki/otocec98.html

Quick, R. (2000). The study finds hope for Internet Retailers. *The Wall Street Journal*, New York, April 18, 2000. Retrieved on February 8, 2002, from the ProQuest database.

Recker, J., & Kathman, J. (2001). The role of consumer in the brand design process. *Design Management Journal, 12*, 70-75, Boston, Summer 2001. Retrieved on February 17, 2004, from the ProQuest database.

Reinhardt, R., & Lott, J. (2002). *Macromedia Flash MX ActionScript bible.* New York: John Wiley & Sons, Inc.

Reichheld, F. F. (1996). *The loyalty effect: The hidden force behind growth, profits, and lasting value.* Boston, MA: Bain & Company, Inc (Harvard Business School Press).

Reiss, E. (2000). *CPR for nonprofits: Creating strategies for successful fundraising, marketing, communications and management.* New York: Addison Wesley Professional.

Roal Pingdom. (2008). How we got from 1 to 162 million websites on the Internet. Retrieved September 9, 2008, from Roal Pingdom website: http:// royal.pingdom.com/tag=www

Robbinson, M., Tapscott, D., & Kalakota, R. (2000). *e-Business 2.0: roadmap for success* (2nd ed.). New York: Addison-Wesley Professional.

Roberts, R. (2001). Aristotle: rhetoric I. Retrieved on December 18, 2002, from the http:// www.molloy.edu/academic/philosophy/sophia/aristotle/rhetoricl a tex.htm.

Roellig, L. (2001). Designing global brands: critical lessons. *Design Management Journal. 12*, 40-45, Boston, Fall 2001. Retrieved on February 17, 2004, from the ProQuest database.

Rutter, J. & Southerton, D. (2000). E-shopping: delivering the goods? *Consumer Policy Review, 10*, 139-144, Manchester, Summer 2000. Retrieved on May 17, 2003, from the ProQuest database.

Sachs, T., & McClain, G. (2002). *Back to the user: creating user-focused Web sites.* New York: New Riders.

Saloner, G., & Spence, M. A. (2002). *Creating and capturing value: perspectives and cases on electronic commerce.* New York: John Wiley & Sons, Inc.

Schiffman, L. G., & Kanuk, L. L. (1994). *Consumer behavior.* (5th ed.). Englewood
    Cliffs, NJ: Simon & Schuster Company.

Schultz, D. E. (2001). Getting to the heart of the brand. *Marketing Management. 10,* 8-
    9, Chicago, Sep/Oct, 2001. Retrieved on February 9, 2003, from the ProQuest
    database.

Schultz, D. E., & Kitchen, P. J. (2001). Global reach. *Adweek,* 41, 51-64, New York,
    Oct 30, 2000. Retrieved February 18, 2002, from the ProQuest database.

Scott, L. M. (1994). Images in advertising: the need for a theory of visual rhetoric. *The
    Journal of Consumer Research. 21,* 252-273.

Sean McManus.com (2003). Keeping your visitors loyal. Retrieved Jun 18, 2003, from
    Sean McManus website: http://www.sean.co.uk/a/webdesign/loyalty.shtm

Shafer, D., & Smith, E. (1997). *NetObjects Fusion 2 design guide: your step-by-step
    project book designing incredible Web pages with NetObjects Fusion 2.* New York:
    The Coriolis Group.

Sindell, K. (2000). *Loyalty marketing for the Internet Age: how to identify, attract,
    serve, and retain customers in an e-commerce environment.* Chicago, IL: Dearborn
    Financial Publishing, Inc.

Smith, M. R. (2000). *e-loyalty: how to keep customers coming back to your Website.*
    New York: Harper Business.

Stallings, W. (2001). *Business data communication.* (4th ed.). Upper Saddle River, NJ:
    Prentice-Hall, Inc.

Stern, B. B. (1997). Advertising intimacy: Relationship making and the services
    consumer. *Journal of Advertising. 26.* Winter 1997.

Sterne, J. (2001). *World Wide Web Marketing: Integrating the Web into your marketing
    strategy* (3rd ed.). New York: John Wiley & Sons, Inc.

Stewart, D. W., Frazier, G. L., & Martin, I. (1996). Integrated channel management:
    merging the communication and distribution functions of the firms. *Integrated
    communication: synergy of persuasive voices,* 185-215. Mahwah, NJ: Lawrence
    Erlbaum Associates.

Stewart, D. W., & Zhao, Q. (2000). Internet marketing, business models, and public policy. *Journal of Public Policy & Marketing*, 19, 287-296, Ann Arbor, Fall 2000. Retrieved December 15, 2002, from the ProQuest database.

Styler, A. (2000). The rules of the marketing game are changing as power shifts to the consumer". *International Journal of Customer Relationship Management*. September/October 2000.

Strauss, J., & Forst, R. (2001). *E-marketing*. NJ: Prentice Hall.

Swaddling, D. C., & Miller, C. (2002). Don't measure customer satisfaction. *Quality Progress*, *35*, 62-67, Milwaukee, May 2002. Retrieved March 26, 2004, from the ProQuest database.

Tabor, S. W. (1999). The customer talks back: an analysis of customer expectations & feedback mechanisms in electronic commerce transactions. *Proceedings of Fifth America Conference on Information Systems*. 553-555, Wisconsin, August 1999.

Taillard, M. (2000). Persuasive communication: the case of marketing. 145-174. Retrieved November 5, 2003, from http://www.phon.ucl.ac.uk/home/PUB/WPL/00papers/taillard.pdf

Terry, S. (1999). The development of online marketplaces or psst, buddy…wanna buy a naked mouse? *Research Report: the portfolio series*, 99-20, July 1999. Retrieved January 18, 2004, from Commerce Net website: http://www.commerce.net/research/ebusiness-strategies/1999/99_20_r.html.

The Economists. (1999). The net imperative: a survey of business and the Internet. Retrieved January 18, 2003, from Economist.com website: http://www.crab.rutgers.edu/~goertzel/economistnetbusiness.html.

Troffer, A. (2000). Writing effectively online: how to compose hypertext: hypertext requires its own rhetoric. Retrieved February 2, 2004, from http://corax.cwrl.utexas.edu/cac/online/o1/troffer/htrhet.html

Van Duyne, D. K., Landay, T. A., & Hong, J. I. (2002). *The design of sites: Patterns, principles, and processes for crafting a customer-centered web experience*. New York: Addison Wesley Professional.

Vine, D. (1995). Executive edge: using the Internet as a strategic business tool. *Internet World*, 44-48, London, January 1995. Retrieved December 15, 2002, from the ProQuest database.

Walton, T. (2002). Exploring the fundamental relationship between design and good business. *Design Management Journal. 13*, 6-10, Boston, Winter 2002. Retrieved April 29, 2002, from the ProQuest database.

Watson, R. T., & Akselsen, S., & Pitt, L. F. (1998). Attractors: building mountains in the flat landscape of the World Wide Web. *California Management Review, 40*, 36-56, Berkeley, Winter 1998. Retrieved July 13, 2003, from http://www.wcu.edu/cob/faculty/schreib/Web_sum02/readings/note%20files/attract ors.pdf

Web-design-uk.biz (2002). Business advantages of using ecommerce. Retrieved Jun 8, 2003, from Web Design UK e-business consultants website: http://www.web-design-uk.biz/ecommerce/business_advantages_of_using_ecommerce.htm

Webster, E. J., & Martocchio, J. J. (1992). Microcomputer playfulness: development of a measure with workplace implications. *MIS Quarterly, 6*, 201-226, Jun 1992. Retrieved July 13, 2003, from http://www.infwest.it.jyu.fi/material/Kokkola25-270403/Vandenbosch/Webster%20et%20al_MIS%20Quaterly%201992,%2016(2). pdf

Whitock, T. (1990). *Metaphor and film.* New York: Cambridge University Press.

Wigand, R.T., & Benjamin, R. I. (1995). Electronic commerce: Effects on electronic markets. Retrieved November 18, 2002, from JCMC website: http://www.ascusc.org/jcmc/vol1/issue3/wigand.html

Williamson, D. A., & Johnson, B. (1995). Web ushers in next generation. *Advertising Age. 13*, May 1995.

Williams, T. R. (2000). Guidelines for designing and evaluating the display of information on the Web. *Technical Communication, 47*, 383-396, Washington, Aug 2000. Retrieved April 20, 2002, from the ProQuest database.

Winn, W., & Beck, K. (2002). The persuasive of design elements on an e-commerce website. *Technical Communication, 3*, 17-35, Washington, Feb 2002. Retrieved April 18, 2002, from the ProQuest database.

Wolak, F. A. (2001). Designing a competitive wholesale electricity market that benefits consumers. Retrieved April 15, 2003, from Stanford University website: http://www-hoover.stanford.edu/research/conferences/calelectricity/wolak.pdf

Wolf, M, J. (1999). *The Entertainment economy: how Mega-Media forces are transforming our lives.* New York: Random House.

Wolfinbarger, M., & Gilly, M. C. (2001). Shopping online for freedom, control, and fun. *California Management Review, 43,* 34-55, Berkely, Winter 2001. Retrieved January 21, 2004, from the ProQuest database.

Zakon, R. H. (2003). Hobbe's Internet timeline v6.0. Retrieved May 18, 2003, from Imaginary Landscape website: http://www.zakon.org/robert/internet/timeline/

Zimmerman, J. (2001). *Marketing on the Internet: seven steps to building the Internet into your business.* Florida: Maximum Press.

**Appendix A**

**The E-mail Invitation Letter**

# THIS RESEARCHER NEEDS YOUR HELP!!!

You are invited to participate in an anonymous Web survey. This research study is entitled, The Persuasive Power of Website Design: Marketing Loyalty in the E-Commerce Environment. Your responses will add significantly to the understanding of consumer behavior in online environments.

**You need to have previous online buying experience on the Internet** to participate in this survey. If you agree to be a participant, please click the hyperlink below:

http://www.mysurvey.hostignition.com/loyalty/

You can also help by forwarding this email to your friends and associates. Thank you very much for helping with my study!


Tsai-Shin Fong
Lynn University

Appendix B

An Information and Informed Consent Statement for Web Participants

# The Persuasive Power of Website Design: Marketing Loyalty
# in the E- Commerce Environment

Tsai-Shin Fong

## An Information and Informed Consent for Participants on This Web Based Research

You are invited to participate in a Web survey for a research study entitled, "The Persuasive Power of Website Design: Marketing Loyalty in the E- Commerce Environment". The research is using a sample of consumers who have previous experience with online products purchases. *Thus, you need to have online buying experience on the Internet to participate in this survey.*

This research is intended to assess online consumers' feelings, thoughts, and attitudes about the website design. If you agree to take part in this research, you will be asked to complete an online questionnaire. The results from this research will help manager's to make the important strategy, quality, and operational decisions that are necessary for effective e-commerce implementation.

Your participation in this research is completely voluntary. By completing this survey, you will help ensure that the researcher will have the best information possible. The survey contains 36 closed-ended questions, plus an open-ended question at the end. Based on preliminary tests, completing the questionnaire will take you approximately 5-7 minutes. You may refuse to participate, discontinue participation, or skip any questions you do not wish to answer at any time without penalty, although the researcher hopes that you respond to all questions. Your answers are completely confidential and the results will only be released as summaries so that no individual's answers can be identified. *By completing and submitting the questionnaire, you give your informed consent to participate in this research.*

If you have any questions about your rights as a participant in this research, please contact with Ms. Tsai-Shin Fong by e-mail at tfong@pop.student.lynn.edu.
Thank you very much for helping with this important research.
Sincerely,

Tsai-Shin Fong
Lynn University

Appendix C

The Consumer Loyalty Questionnaire (Paper Version)

## The Consumer Loyalty Questionnaire

**Survey Instructions**

Please follow the directions below to complete this survey.

- In answering all of the questions, please use a scale from 1 to 9 **where 1 means "very strongly disagree", 5 means "neither agree nor disagree", and 9 means "very strongly agree".** Write a number in the space provided that best indicate your feelings about the question.

---

*Section 1*

Rate the following questions from 1 to 9. Please use the scale as explained in the survey instructions.
In this section, please **DO NOT USE THE SAME NUMBER MORE THAN ONCE!**

- I would likely make repeated purchases from the website:

1. ___ if it offers various choices of products to me.
2. ___ if it can easily help me to quickly find the product that I want.

---

*Section 2*

Rate the following questions from 1 to 9. Please use the scale as explained in the survey instructions.
In this section, please **DO NOT USE THE SAME NUMBER MORE THAN ONCE!**

- I would likely make repeated purchases from the website:

3. ___ if it shows me its discount prices.
4. ___ if it shows me any potential savings.
5. ___ if it lets me know the shipping fees of each product before I click it into the shopping cart.
6. ___ if it shows me comparisons with competitors' prices.

---

*Section 3*

Rate the following questions from 1 to 9. Please use the scale as explained in the survey instructions.
In this section, please **DO NOT USE THE SAME NUMBER MORE THAN ONCE!**

- I would likely make repeated purchases from the website:

7. ___ if it offers very detailed product information to me.
8. ___ if it offers up-to-date product information to me.
9. ___ if it makes all product information easy to find and read.

---------------------------------------------------------------------------------

*Section 4*

Rate the following questions from 1 to 9. Please use the scale as explained in the survey instructions.
In this section, please **DO NOT USE THE SAME NUMBER MORE THAN ONCE!**

- I would likely make repeated purchases from the website:

10. ___ if it offers clear and understandable links for moving around the Web
site.
11. ___ if I am able to complete my online shopping with little or no difficulty.

---------------------------------------------------------------------------------

*Section 5*

Rate the following questions from 1 to 9. Please use the scale as explained in the survey instructions.
In this section, please **DO NOT USE THE SAME NUMBER MORE THAN ONCE!**

- I would likely make repeated purchases from the website:

12. ___ if it offers me entertaining elements such as: games.
13. ___ if it offers me entertaining elements such as: jokes.
14. ___ if it offers me entertaining elements such as: cartoons.
15. ___ if it changes entertaining elements frequently.

---------------------------------------------------------------------------------

*Section 6*

Rate the following questions from 1 to 9. Please use the scale as explained in the survey instructions.
In this section, please **DO NOT USE THE SAME NUMBER MORE THAN ONCE!**

- I would likely make repeated purchases from the website:

16. ___ if it has many colorful pictures to help me make my purchase decision.
17. ___ if it has audio effects (e.g., music or voices).
18. ___ if it offers me a video film to observe the product (e.g., 3D virtual tour).

---------------------------------------------------------------------------------

Rate the following questions from 1 to 9. Please use the scale as explained in the survey instructions.
In this section, please **DO NOT USE THE SAME NUMBER MORE THAN ONCE!**

• I would likely make repeated purchases from the website:

19. ___ if it has a strong corporate image that I recognize.

20. ___ if it includes many product brands that are familiar to me.

---

*Section 8*

Rate the following questions from 1 to 9. Please use the scale as explained in the survey instructions.
In this section, please **DO NOT USE THE SAME NUMBER MORE THAN ONCE!**

• I would likely make repeated purchases from the website:

21. ___ if it offers me connections to other buyers of this product (i.e. through bulletin
boards or chat rooms).

22. ___ if it offers electronic newsletters to me.

---

*Section 9*

Rate the following questions from 1 to 9. Please use the scale as explained in the survey instructions.
In this section, please **DO NOT USE THE SAME NUMBER MORE THAN ONCE!**

• I would likely make repeated purchases from the website:

23. ___ if it learns my personal buying pattern and offers me more
useful purchasing information based on that learning.

24. ___ if it includes clear statements assuring my privacy and security.

---

*Section 10*

Rate the following questions from 1 to 9. Please use the scale as explained in the survey instructions.
In this section, please **DO NOT USE THE SAME NUMBER MORE THAN ONCE!**

• I would likely make repeated purchases from the website:

25. ___ if I was ensured that the company offers good customer service.

26. ___ if it includes delivery tracking information.

27. ___ if it has a clear delivery time schedule.

28. ___ if it includes a policy for returning items.

29. ___ if it offers an e-mail link to communicate with the company.

30. ___ if it offers a 1-800 phone number to communicate with the company.

-------------------------------------------------------------------------------

*Section 11*

Rate the following questions from 1 to 9. Please use the scale as explained in the survey instructions.
In this section, please **DO NOT USE THE SAME NUMBER MORE THAN ONCE!**

31. ___ I would visit the website more frequently if that website met my
    expectations.

32. ___ I would more likely recommend the website to my friends if that website met
    my expectations.

33. ___ I would more likely make repeated purchases from the website if that website
    met my purchasing needs.

-------------------------------------------------------------------------------

**Please write your responds regarding your basic information.**

34. ___ What is your age?

35. Are you female or male? (Please check one)

    1 ☐ Female

    2 ☐ Male

36. What is your highest level of education? (Please check one)

    1 ☐ Vocational

    2 ☐ High school degree

    3 ☐ College degree

    4 ☐ Master degree

$_5\square$    Doctoral degree

37. Do you have any additional suggestions regarding website design? Please write below:

```



```

**Please click the submit button after you finish the questionnaire!**

**Thanks again for your time in helping with this research!**

**Appendix D**

**The Consumer Loyalty Questionnaire (Web Version)**

# The Consumer Loyalty Questionnaire

Please follow the steps below to complete this survey.

- In answering all of the questions, please **use a scale from 1 to 9** where 1 means "very strongly disagree", 5 means "neither agree nor disagree", and 9 means "very strongly agree". Write a number in the space provided that best indicate your feelings about the question.

|  1 | 5 | 9 |
| --- | --- | --- |
| very strongly disagree | neither agree nor disagree | very strongly agree |

---

*Section 1*

Rate the following questions from 1 to 9. Please use the scale as explained in the survey instructions. In this section, please DO NOT USE THE SAME NUMBER MORE THAN ONCE!

**I would likely to make repeated purchases from the Web site:**

1. if it offers various choices of products to me.

2. if it can easily help me to quickly find the product that I want.

---

*Section 2*

Rate the following questions from 1 to 9. Please use the scale as explained in the survey instructions. In this section, please DO NOT USE THE SAME NUMBER MORE THAN ONCE!

**I would likely to make repeated purchases from the Web site:**

3. if it shows me its discount prices.

4. if it shows me any potential savings.

5. if it lets me know the shipping fees of each product before I click it into the shopping cart.

        6.   if it shows me comparisons with competitors' prices.

. . . . . . . . . . . . . . . . . . . . . . . . . . . . . . . . . . . . . . . . . . . . . . . . . . . . . . . . . . . . . . . . . . . . . . . . . . . . . . . . . . . . . . . . . . . . .

*Section 3*

Rate the following questions from 1 to 9. Please use the scale as explained in the survey instructions. In this section, please DO NOT USE THE SAME NUMBER MORE THAN ONCE!

**I would likely to make repeated purchases from the Web site:**

        7.   if it offers very detailed product information to me.

        8.   if it offers up-to-date product information to me.

        9.   if it makes all product information easy to find and read.

. . . . . . . . . . . . . . . . . . . . . . . . . . . . . . . . . . . . . . . . . . . . . . . . . . . . . . . . . . . . . . . . . . . . . . . . . . . . . . . . . . . . . . . . . . . . .

*Section 4*

Rate the following questions from 1 to 9. Please use the scale as explained in the survey instructions. In this section, please DO NOT USE THE SAME NUMBER MORE THAN ONCE!

**I would likely to make repeated purchases from the Web site:**

        10.  if it offers clear and understandable links for moving around the Web site.

        11.  if I am able to complete my online shopping with little or no difficulty.

. . . . . . . . . . . . . . . . . . . . . . . . . . . . . . . . . . . . . . . . . . . . . . . . . . . . . . . . . . . . . . . . . . . . . . . . . . . . . . . . . . . . . . . . . . . . .

*Section 5*

Rate the following questions from 1 to 9. Please use the scale as explained in the survey instructions. In this section, please DO NOT USE THE SAME NUMBER MORE THAN ONCE!

**I would likely to make repeated purchases from the Web site:**

        12.  if it offers me entertaining elements such as: games.

        13.  if it offers me entertaining elements such as: jokes.

        14.  if it offers me entertaining elements such as: cartoons.

15. if it changes entertaining elements frequently.

---

*Section 6*

Rate the following questions from 1 to 9. Please use the scale as explained in the survey instructions. In this section, please DO NOT USE THE SAME NUMBER MORE THAN ONCE!

**I would likely to make repeated purchases from the Web site:**

16. if it has many colorful pictures to help me make my purchase decision.

17. if it has audio effects (e.g., music or voices).

18. if it offers me a video film to observe the product (e.g., 3D virtual tour).

---

*Section 7*

Rate the following questions from 1 to 9. Please use the scale as explained in the survey instructions. In this section, please DO NOT USE THE SAME NUMBER MORE THAN ONCE!

**I would likely to make repeated purchases from the Web site:**

19. if it has a strong corporate image that I recognize.

20. if it includes many product brands that are familiar to me.

---

*Section 8*

Rate the following questions from 1 to 9. Please use the scale as explained in the survey instructions. In this section, please DO NOT USE THE SAME NUMBER MORE THAN ONCE!

**I would likely to make repeated purchases from the Web site:**

21. if it offers me connections to other buyers of this product (i.e. through bulletin boards or chat rooms).

22. if it offers electronic newsletters to me.

---

*Section 9*

Rate the following questions from 1 to 9. Please use the scale as explained in the survey instructions. In this section, please DO NOT USE THE SAME NUMBER MORE THAN ONCE!

**I would likely to make repeated purchases from the Web site:**

23. if it learns my personal buying pattern and offers me more useful purchasing information based on that learning.

24. if it includes clear statements assuring my privacy and security.

---

Rate the following questions from 1 to 9. Please use the scale as explained in the survey instructions. In this section, please DO NOT USE THE SAME NUMBER MORE THAN ONCE!

**I would likely to make repeated purchases from the Web site:**

25. if I was ensured that the company offers good customer service.

26. if it includes delivery tracking information.

27. if it has a clear delivery time schedule.

28. if it includes a policy for returning items.

29. if it offers an e-mail link to communicate with the company.

30. if it offers a 1-800 phone number to communicate with the company.

---

*Section 11*

Rate the following questions from 1 to 9. Please use the scale as explained in the survey instructions. In this section, please DO NOT USE THE SAME NUMBER MORE THAN ONCE!

31. I would visit the Web site more frequently if that Web site met my expectations.

32. I would more likely recommend the Web site to my friends if that Web site met my expectations.

33. I would more likely make repeated purchases from the Web site if that Web site met my purchasing needs.

---

**Please write in the answer about your basic information.**

34. What is your age?  |                    |

35. Are you female or male? (Please check one)
    ☐ Female
    ☐ Male

36. What is your highest level of education? (Please check one)
    ☐ Vocational
    ☐ High school degree
    ☐ College degree
    ☐ Master degree
    ☐ Doctoral degree

37 Do you have any additional suggestions regarding Web site design? Please write below:

Please click the submit button after you finish the questionnaire!
Thanks again for your time in helping with this research!

SUBMIT ◉

**Appendix E**

**The Result of Correlation Coefficient between Eleven Sub-Independent Variables**

| | | Variety | Price | Information | Effort | Playfulness | Tangibility | LOYALTY |
|---|---|---|---|---|---|---|---|---|
| Variety | | 1 | .176** | .421** | .381** | .007 | .178** | .529** |
| | Sig. | | .002 | .000 | .000 | .896 | .002 | .000 |
| Price | | .176** | 1 | .094 | .151** | .057 | .067 | .332** |
| | Sig. | .002 | . | .101 | .008 | .317 | .245 | .000 |
| Information | | .421** | .094 | 1 | .404** | .086 | .248** | .508** |
| | Sig. | .000 | .101 | . | .000 | .132 | .000 | .000 |
| Effort | | .381** | .151** | .404** | 1 | .058 | .349** | .549** |
| | Sig. | .000 | .008 | .000 | . | .308 | .000 | .000 |
| Playfulness | | .007 | .057 | .086 | .058 | 1 | .254** | .041 |
| | Sig. | .896 | .317 | .132 | .308 | . | .000 | .475 |
| Tangiblility | | .178** | .067 | .248** | .349** | .254** | 1 | .408** |
| | Sig. | .002 | .245 | .000 | .000 | .000 | . | .000 |
| Empathy | | .246** | .132* | .338** | .414** | .242** | .519** | .475** |
| | Sig. | .000 | .021 | .000 | .000 | .000 | .000 | .000 |
| Recognizability | | .367** | .295** | .417** | .364** | .107 | .304** | .564** |
| | Sig. | .000 | .000 | .000 | .000 | .061 | .000 | .000 |
| Compatibility | | .072 | .032 | .222** | .352** | .168** | .480** | .341** |
| | Sig. | .209 | .577 | .000 | .000 | .003 | .000 | .000 |
| Assurance | | .164** | .196** | .171** | .264** | .027 | .159** | .356** |
| | Sig. | .004 | .001 | .003 | .000 | .634 | .005 | .000 |
| Reliability | | .209** | .251** | .297** | .182** | .029 | .121* | .363** |
| | Sig. | .000 | .000 | .000 | .001 | .612 | .034 | .000 |
| LOYALTY | | .529** | .332** | .508** | .549** | .041 | .408** | 1 |
| | Sig. | .000 | .000 | .000 | .000 | .475 | .000 | . |

**. Correlation is significant at the 0.01 level (2-tailed).

*. Correlation is significant at the 0.05 level (2-tailed).

**Pearson Correlations**

| | | Empathy | Recognizability | Compatibility | Assurance | Reliability | LOYALTY |
|---|---|---|---|---|---|---|---|
| Variety | | .246** | .367** | .072 | .164** | .209** | .529** |
| | Sig. | .000 | .000 | .209 | .004 | .000 | .000 |
| Price | | .132* | .295** | .032 | .196** | .251** | .332** |
| | Sig. | .021 | .000 | .577 | .001 | .000 | .000 |
| Information | | .338** | .417** | .222** | .171** | .297** | .508** |
| | Sig. | .000 | .000 | .000 | .003 | .000 | .000 |
| Effort | | .414** | .364** | .352** | .264** | .182** | .549** |
| | Sig. | .000 | .000 | .000 | .000 | .001 | .000 |
| Playfulness | | .242** | .107 | .168** | .027 | .029 | .041 |
| | Sig. | .000 | .061 | .003 | .634 | .612 | .475 |
| Tangiblility | | .519** | .304** | .480** | .159** | .121* | .408** |
| | Sig. | .000 | .000 | .000 | .005 | .034 | .000 |
| Empathy | | 1 | .358** | .385** | .248** | .207** | .475** |
| | Sig. | . | .000 | .000 | .000 | .000 | .000 |
| Recognizability | | .358** | 1 | .244** | .250** | .230** | .564** |
| | Sig. | .000 | . | .000 | .000 | .000 | .000 |
| Compatibility | | .385** | .244** | 1 | .105 | .053 | .341** |
| | Sig. | .000 | .000 | . | .067 | .356 | .000 |
| Assurance | | .248** | .250** | .105 | 1 | .170** | .356** |
| | Sig. | .000 | .000 | .067 | . | .003 | .000 |
| Reliability | | .207** | .230** | .053 | .170** | 1 | .363** |
| | Sig. | .000 | .000 | .356 | .003 | . | .000 |
| LOYALTY | | .475** | .564** | .341** | .356** | .363** | 1 |
| | Sig. | .000 | .000 | .000 | .000 | .000 | . |

**. Correlation is significant at the 0.01 level (2-tailed).

*. Correlation is significant at the 0.05 level (2-tailed).

Appendix F

ANOVA Analysis: Descriptive Information of Each Age Group

**Descriptives**

LOGOS

|  | Mean | Std. Deviation | Std. Error | Minimum | Maximum |
|---|---|---|---|---|---|
| 1 | 7.290 | .4994 | .0497 | 5.9 | 8.0 |
| 2 | 7.263 | .4969 | .0485 | 5.3 | 8.2 |
| 3 | 7.413 | .5438 | .0727 | 5.4 | 8.1 |
| 4 | 7.158 | .5157 | .0769 | 5.6 | 8.0 |
| Total | 7.284 | .5122 | .0292 | 5.3 | 8.2 |

1= 18-22 years, 2= 23-35 years, 3= 36-50 years, 4= 51 or older.

**Descriptives**

PATHOS

|  | Mean | Std. Deviation | Std. Error | Minimum | Maximum |
|---|---|---|---|---|---|
| 1 | 6.433 | .7382 | .0735 | 4.9 | 8.0 |
| 2 | 6.072 | .7578 | .0740 | 3.6 | 7.5 |
| 3 | 5.617 | .6241 | .0834 | 4.4 | 7.2 |
| 4 | 4.711 | .7859 | .1172 | 3.1 | 6.5 |
| Total | 5.909 | .9266 | .0529 | 3.1 | 8.0 |

1= 18-22 years, 2= 23-35 years, 3= 36-50 years, 4= 51 or older.

**Descriptives**

ETHOS

|  | Mean | Std. Deviation | Std. Error | Minimum | Maximum |
|---|---|---|---|---|---|
| 1 | 7.375 | .5121 | .0510 | 5.8 | 8.3 |
| 2 | 7.232 | .6082 | .0594 | 5.1 | 8.4 |
| 3 | 7.258 | .5669 | .0758 | 5.3 | 8.2 |
| 4 | 6.606 | .6766 | .1009 | 5.3 | 8.0 |
| Total | 7.192 | .6309 | .0360 | 5.1 | 8.4 |

1= 18-22 years, 2= 23-35 years, 3= 36-50 years, 4= 51 or older.

**Appendix G**

**The Open-ended Question: Comments by Subjects**

- Subject 7: Tell companies I will not buy from pop ups. I think most of Websites are too cluttered.

- Subject 13: Websites should be user-friendly, but it's also important that you are able to speak to someone if you have a problem. So often, when you deal with websites, your only option is to communicate via e-mail.

- Subject 15: Ease of navigation is important; also, clear shipping information is good to know.

- Subject 17: I appreciate fast service from the site.

- Subject 36: My repeated purchases have been for services, not products. For those purchases, I have most often used the provider's web-site, not an intermediary service that sells on behalf of the company. But, I use those other sites sometimes to get a sense of pricing.

- Subject 38: I feel that the most important aspect of purchasing through a website is for it to offer quick, easy, and clear navigation for the consumer. From my own experience, if I don't receive this to my satisfaction, I will not purchase a second time from them.

- Subject 42: I hate junk mails! I need my privacy; please do not sell my e-mail address or personal information to any company.

- Subject 46: I like online auctions where there are time limits for buying and selling items. To me, that is the best design for buying and selling items because you then pay or receive what the market will bear.

- Subject 64: Assurance from company is to guarantee complete satisfaction or money back guarantee, complete with shipping and handling coverage for returned items.

- Subject 67: I like a colorful and aesthetically pleasing Web design. However, it is better to lack of pop-up ads (very annoying).

- Subject 78: When using the Internet, safety, and speed of delivery are my priority consideration.

- Subject 79: The only suggestion would be to make sure that I was not put on a mailing list, as the one thing that would drive me away from a business is getting spammed with e-mail offers and being put on mailing lists for things I was never interested in, in the first place.

- Subject 93: Simple, easy to use. Most importantly, an easy simple way to "talk" with or back to the company. In almost every instance when I have had problems with an e-commerce Website, it has been very frustrating trying to get through to the company. I very strongly feel that every website should have a supporting 800 number if the email connection doesn't work.

- Subject 94: Fast, on-time delivery and customer service is more important to me than the design of the website.

- Subject 104: I think the primary value of a Web design is clarity. It is better to avoid distracting "bells and whistles".

- Subject 111: I think websites that are selling high end merchandise such as automobiles should offer a live chat or video conference option to potential buyers.

- Subject 131: In general, I feel that the "feel" of a website is more important than the "look" of a website. In other words, navigation logicalness is preferred over fancy graphics or multi-media content.

- Subject 161: Having advertisements for other companies are very distracting and many things on one page can become confusing.

- Subject 178: For sites that aren't name-brand, I rely on recommendations and ratings of other users.

- Subject 262: My biggest frustration is that I do not know approximate shipping charges until very late in the ordering process.

- Subject 283: Don't make me think too much! Learn my personal shopping style.

www.ingramcontent.com/pod-product-compliance
Lightning Source LLC
LaVergne TN
LVHW022309060326
832902LV00020B/3353

* 9 7 8 3 6 3 9 0 8 4 2 9 0 *